D1630322

"The longest running couple in the world."
(Ffyona Campbell)

Husband and wife, Richard and Sandra Brown, are the world's greatest long distance running and walking couple. They both have world and many UK records. Richard has successfully completed over 75 events of 100 miles or more since he took up ultra distance racing in 1983. He has also held senior management positions in both the public and private sectors. Sandra is a senior Treasury official in Whitehall. They have a daughter, Victoria.

Dedicated to

Sandra

and our support crews; together we broke the Land's End to John O'Groats records:

Van 1:	Van 2:	Van 3	Van 4
Doug	**Amos**	**Boyd**	**Jill/Dave**
James	**Don**	**Glenys**	**Sue**
Debbie	**Derek**	**Roy**	**Roger**
Ian	**Cyril**	**John/Lucy**	**Liz**

Plus Annie and Claire

Copyright© Richard Brown 1996

All rights reserved. No part of this publication
may be reproduced, stored in a retrieval system,
or transmitted in any form or by any means,
electronic, mechanical, photocopying, recording,
or otherwise without the prior permission of the publishers.

Published in Great Britain in 1996 by
Institute of Human Development
Burnts House
Chelwood
BS18 4NL

Typeset by Sue Sheppard - The No 1 Staff Bureau, Bristol
Illustrations set by Strange and Dawson Advertising, Bristol
Printed and bound in the UK by
Redwood Books, Trowbridge, Wilts

ISBN 0 9527437 02

THE
WINNING
EXPERIENCE

Winning:
- **– in sport**
- **– in business**
- **– in life**

RICHARD BROWN

Institute of Human Development

Contents

1

Introduction

I suppose for everyone there are a few great moments in life. Moments we look back on and draw warmth and exhilaration from, even though they may have happened years ago.

Such moments don't just happen. They require effort. You have to go and create them. Making the effort is part of the achievement. None of us know what we're really capable of achieving until we make that effort. Too often we are afraid; afraid to dream dreams, to think what we might achieve, to set ourselves goals and ambitions and then set about realising them. We are afraid of failing; afraid of exploring not just the outer world but also our inner self; of pushing out our boundaries of experience; of delving deep into ourselves and tapping the creativity and potential which exists in all of us in our own different ways. We waste our potential without even realising it because we don't bother to find out what exists within us.

David Hemmery, a great Olympic hurdler, said many years ago that we can achieve anything within the scope of our imagination. *"We simply don't often dare to dream what we might achieve in our lives."*

This book I hope shows how two ordinary people with no great talent but with considerable determination and belief, dreamed a dream and then went out and lived it. It could have been any dream, any vision. It happened to be setting a unique double: breaking both the men's and women's Lands End to John O'Groats running records.

The particular achievement is however less significant than the approach adopted and the lessons learned. How to set a vision and then develop the action plans and team approach and the mental determination to reach the target set is relevant for any organisation and any individual wanting to succeed.

But how many of us set ourselves long term goals, believe in them and really get down to achieving them? We can all dream about what might be, or more usually and negatively - about what might have been. But how often do we sit down quietly and work out what we would really like to achieve in our lives? Do we decide for example what balance we want between work, outside interests, our families, local communities and friends and helping those less fortunate than ourselves? Or is the agenda set by others, with work taking an ever greater share and the rest somehow being fitted in? If this is the case, whose fault is it? How many of us are likely to say at the end of our lives: "I wish I had spent more time at work"?

We must achieve a better sense of balance and a more satisfying wholeness in our lives.

We need to create our own personal development plan. Companies have plans as to how they aim to achieve their objectives. We need the same approach. We should set out what we want from life, what we will contribute to it and how we aim to balance achievement in one area with achievement in another area. We should think about and plan how we will continue to learn, to increase our skills and hence face the uncertain future with greater confidence. We can take greater control of our lives.

I hope no one who reads this book will say of the future "If only I had done that," "If only I had seized that opportunity." From now on your life can be more under your own influence as you set about achieving what you really want.

This book will help you secure a more satisfying and lasting success in business, in sport or in any other area you may choose which is important to you. It covers many of the basic principles of organisational success such as:
- self analysis and awareness
- setting stretching but realistic goals
- creating a winning team
- achieving success even when the going gets tough.

It also, I hope, covers these in a friendly, practical way drawing on the Land's End to John O'Groats experience as an example.

Too many management books set out to try and prove a thesis or in some other way clothe, obscure and mystify what are basically simple concepts. By placing the themes which should be followed by good managers (including good self-managers) anywhere in an athletics context, I have tried to demystify them.

But to make even the most simple concept come alive requires a belief in our own ability to make things happen. Hence the central recurring theme in this book is how to develop that winning mentality, that belief in the vast untapped potential that exists in every one of us which distinguishes achievers from the rest. Each of us has to decide how much of that potential we will realise and how much we will let go to waste.

To realise our potential, we will have to leave behind the baggage of fears and doubts we have been carrying around. We must have the confidence to draw strength from within, to look forward positively and enthusiastically whatever our age or abilities. Success is an attitude of mind.

We must also learn not to measure ourselves against the achievements of others but rather against our own potential. We know when we are giving our best, when we are proud of what we have achieved, when we have given pleasure to others unselfishly and unstintingly. We must set the standards. We must climb the hill we have set before us and, when we have reached the top, look for new challenges, new excitements, new opportunities.

By the time you have read this book, I hope you will have set yourself a clear path towards a new vision on a hill ahead with a deeper understanding of yourself, and a renewed commitment and zest for life. I hope you will set exciting challenges for yourself this year, this month, this week. I hope you will not only dream your dreams but also have the new found confidence to go out and live them with fun, a belief in self-achievement, a sense of The Winning Experience.

2

The Land's End
to John O'Groats Challenge

The journey from Land's End to John O'Groats holds a fascination for many people. Travelling from one end of Britain to the other is a journey with a definable start and finish, a definite purpose with an end in view. Going round in circles on a marathon run or even covering the 55 miles from London to Brighton in a veteran car or bike or on foot does not have the same sense of challenge and adventure. The "End to End" has an aura and even a finality about it.

Maybe that is why in the height of the season around 20 hopefuls can set out each day from either the North or the South to make the journey. Many will be on motorbikes or in cars, on pedal bikes or on foot. Some will be more eccentric and walk backwards, bounce balls or balance on a uniped.

There is something in the blood that makes all that set out take up the challenge. It is not just a sense of adventure, of travelling for travelling's sake, or of wanting to explore the varied countryside. There is also something of that inner need which takes people on pilgrimages. It is a feeling of wanting to satisfy some restless drive, to explore a deeper self and experience something unique and far removed from what we can achieve in the rush of everyday life.

Medieval pilgrims no doubt had a similar mixture of feelings. Their quest was not just for spiritual rewards and remissions of time in purgatory. Their journeys had a social and personal dimension with some deep calling and a sense of mission, underlying their long journeys. It was no doubt this inner resolve which helped them withstand great privations in their journeys to the shrine of St James at Santiago de Compostella in Northern Spain, or to Rome or, even more so, to the Holy Land. They often travelled in convoy for protection but were still prone to bandits and unscrupulous innkeepers, sailors and traders as well as sickness and uncertainty as to when or even whether they would return.

That spirit of adventure and personal quest has continued down the ages. It was in 1882 that two Leeds policemen began the great trek from one end of Britain to the other on penny farthing bicycles. Considering their mode of transport and the state of the "roads," their time of 14 days was a remarkable achievement. When Billy Butlin decided to organise a mass go-as-you-please foot race from John O'Groats to Land's End in February 1960, no less than 4,000 people answered the advertisement, 1,500 sent in entry forms and, despite appalling weather, 715 actually started. They had to contend with snow, very cold rain, sleet and freezing conditions all the way down to the finish.

The interest in such a journey had been engendered by an eccentric Russian-born scientist dietician, Dr Barbara Moore. Her aim was to show that such demanding activities could be accomplished on a diet largely composed of fruit juices, honey and green vegetables. She was one of the first great advocates of vegetarianism and in the late 1950s her red polka dot head scarf, black cardigan and navy slacks could be seen on various routes including the 100 mile road from Birmingham to London and the 373 mile walk from Edinburgh to London.

"Dr Babs" duly completed the John O'Groats to Land's End (a distance of around 1000 miles by the route she chose) in 23 days. She averaged about 4 miles per hours for eleven hours a day.

The Billy Butlin epic was won by James Musgrave (a 37 year old Doncaster glass worker) who covered the 891 miles route in 15 days, 14 hours and 31 minutes. Wendy Lewis (a hairdresser) won the ladies event in 17 days 7 hours and 30 minutes, just 6 hours ahead of Beryl Randle (a future redoubtable force in British athletics administration). All three received £1,000.

The second man John Grundy (who had led for much of the race and finished just 1 hour 23 minutes behind Musgrave) received £500. This was an interesting reversal of the regime of higher funding for male athletes which women had subsequently to fight against. As a result of his money, John Grundy was banned from amateur athletics and only reinstated in the 1980s when the fiction of amateurism was finally abandoned.

Meanwhile, back along the icy route stretched the remains of this epic race. In the words of Peter Lovesey (author of a marvellous detective story "Wobble to Death" which is set against the background of a 6 day ultra distance run):

"The snowbound north of Scotland witnessed the greatest gathering of eccentrics since Peter the Hermit's crusade. For months afterwards hospitals along the race route were littered with the human debris of Butlin's extravaganza."

Questions were asked in Parliament about the cost to the public of all the injured, though Billy Butlin himself evidently paid for many destitute competitors to return home.

According to Andy Milroy, Billy Butlin probably recognised that such a mass event was unmanageable and perhaps too expensive to repeat. Within a few days of the start, for example, three hundred had retired and one hundred been disqualified for taking lifts. Additional secret check points were subsequently added.

The event nevertheless captured the public's imagination and was a major influence on the development of the Land's End to John O'Groats route as a great challenge to be attempted by conventional and unconventional modes of transport.

The men's record was slowly reduced over the years and was claimed by Fred Hicks in May 1977 as 10 days 3 hours 30 minutes. Doubts however surrounded this claim and it was never authenticated. Thus in 1988 the allcomers record officially rested with the South African Ken Craig at 12 hours 1 minute 15 seconds. This had been set in August 1984 with the UK record of 12 days 8 hours and 43 minutes set by Colin Dixon in July 1985.

It was in September of that year that I set out with a support team of 7 in two camper vans to lower this record. After a great start with 90 miles on the first day, 85 on the second and 80 on the third, we made somewhat erratic progress with injuries to my calf muscles as well as the inevitable blisters slowing me sometimes to a painful crawl. In driving rain and a northwesterly wind, we finally however made it in the early hours to the sign that announces:

"John O'Groats
The Last House
Souvenirs and Postcards."

We had lowered the record to 10 days 18 hours 23 minutes.

I knew I had made the big time when I was interviewed on the Radio 1 lunchtime news! My father happened to be in his local library when someone said, "A chap has just broken the Land's End to John O'Groats running record." Dad responded, "Yes, that's my son." No doubt he felt even taller that his six feet!

We had learnt a lot from the experience and I felt I could lower the record further to at least 10½ days and perhaps even to around 10 days given a following wind (literally!). Looking at the previous attempts (particularly the Barbara Moore and Billy Butlin exploits) also made me feel I was comparatively sane and ordinary. But then all things are relative!

However, the following spring, the great 100km runner Don Ritchie lowered my record by under 3 hours. It was his third attempt at the run. Previous efforts had been thwarted by injury.

Don's approach had been very different to mine. We had each played to our strengths. I had relied on my walking to maintain a steady and economical pace. I had run down many of the hills to maintain a good daily average and to use the different muscles which walking and running deploy. But a reliance on walking meant I had to remain on my feet for many more hours to cover a respectable daily mileage. I ate and drank as I went and hence was reliant on my support team to look after me.

Don, by contrast, had run 3 marathons a day at a fairly fast pace and interspersed his bouts of running with long rest periods when he had eaten and slept. His time on his feet was probably about 10 hours per day against my 17 hours.

I knew I could lower the record by a respectable margin but I had to wait 6 years before I could mount the attempt.

The ladies record had been lowered to 13 days 18 hours 10 minutes by the formidable Ann Sayer in 1983. It was in fact a walking record which had never been beaten by any runner. Ann was a good friend and rightly proud of her long standing achievement. It was, however, time for someone to have a real go at it. What better challenger than the person who had taken over Ann's mantle as the UK's premier women's long distance walker, indeed the greatest long distance race walker in the world, my wife Sandra.

She was just as capable as I was of lowering the overall record of 10 days 15 hours 20 minutes. That was one reason why our joint assault would be so intriguing. Who would get there first?

3

The First Steps

"Success is more attitude than aptitude."
It is so easy to think of reasons why someone else should be successful and to make excuses as to why it is not worth making an effort yourself.

"Well, of course he's a natural athlete ... she is so slim ... he has his father's head for figures ... she has her mother's charm."

We have all heard and no doubt made excuses as to why someone else is better or more successful than we are. The negatives, the weaknesses, the risks of taking control of our own lives are so often accentuated and blind us to the positive, the strengths and the potential which exist in all of us.

We are conditioned at an early age to "be careful," to "not do that," to "play safe," to "let me do that, it's too difficult for you." The fun of exploration, the joy of discovery, the pleasure of sharing achievements with others can so easily be dampened.

But it need not be. We hold within us the key to unlock again the door into that secret garden, to find delight in new adventures and pleasures and to delve into our own selves to find again both the hopes and pleasures which excited us as children and discover those new capabilities which have been built on our more recent experiences.

We may not be certain where to start at first, but, like a child, we can experiment. We can find things that give us pleasure, activities that we want to engage in, things which we find we are actually quite good at. We can surprise ourselves. We may find that what we like, we become good at and vice versa. We are finding out more about ourselves. We are doing our own thing, developing along a natural path through following our own instincts. That is the way to find and ultimately realise our own potential. That was how it was with Sandra and me.

During our twenties, our walking - and our idea of a holiday - only slowly embraced energetic strolls and eventually whole days in for example the Cairngorms, the Lake District, Dartmoor or Snowdonia. When we could afford to go abroad, we walked and cycled in France and Northern Spain including in the Pyrenees. There was nothing unusually athletic about us. There were no fell runs before breakfast.

Our first experiment in organised athletics was running the Winchester marathon on an icy day early in March 1981. I thought Sandra had entered us for the half marathon. It was only when we got to the start and were putting our clothes in the organisers' black refuse sacks, that Sandra broke the news that we were going all the way.

Since the course was two laps I resolved to pack in after the first circuit. When I had finished the second circuit in under 4 hours, I just sank thankfully to the ground and vowed never to do it again. Sandra shortly appeared in the suitably elegant attire of a pair of small men's football shorts, some gym shoes from a Scout shop, a lady's vest (the underwear variety) and a sort of track jacket ... for modesty's sake!

Thus ill equipped for the Marathon adventure and knowing nothing at all about warming-up or down, stretching, dehydration, pacing etc, etc, it is hardly surprising that we felt incapacitated. But within a day or two like so many people we felt invigorated and looking for the next challenge.

This turned out to be a long-distance challenge event in a lovely area of Dorset. The "Purbeck Plod" is a 24 mile walk and run along coastal paths which have the dreadful habit of going up and down. Sandra entered this event and this time could not tempt me to join her. By the time she had completed, she had heard about the Long Distance Walkers' Association (LDWA) and had her signature on an application form. Somehow I was persuaded to put my signature on another form and meekly agreed to undertake cross-country challenge events that, like the "Purbeck Plod," generally start at 25 miles and go upwards.

But what wonderful events they turned out to be; what tremendous views and countryside which you would never have experienced for yourself, and what great support and friendship from other LDWA members and those manning checkpoints to give you the magic re-invigorating elixirs of rice pudding, fruit cake and warm Ribena. For a day in the hills which will push out the limits of what you find you can achieve, join the LDWA!

Not that every event is a piece of cake (as it were!). I remember the "Dorset Doddle" - which is certainly not a doddle. The event is around 33 miles all over the cliffs from Weymouth to Swanage where you are totally exposed to the elements. One year it can be boiling hot, the next year pouring with rain and with a cold wind off the sea.

One year I thought I'd be clever and run it in just shorts and a singlet, relying on the check-points for support. This was because the previous year it had been blazing hot and I had got sun-burnt all down my right side - the side exposed to the sea and the sun.

Unfortunately, by the time we started, the clouds were coming over, and then it began to drizzle and the wind got up. Although it didn't deteriorate too much, by the time I had done 25 miles I was, as they say, knackered!

I collapsed on the path going up a steep cliff, and just lay there in a daze, wondering what would become of me, and whether anybody would find me on this particular section of the path.

Eventually I staggered on all fours up the cliff. As my head emerged over the top, I could see two old people sitting on a bench, enjoying their sandwiches, and looking out to sea. (It had stopped raining by this time). I continued to crawl towards them, and plaintively asked if they could possible spare me a biscuit.

They hurriedly offered me a couple of cheese sandwiches, packed up their own, and retreated in haste, inland. They were probably fearful of this apparition, and only too anxious to appease the terrible spirit with an offering, in the hope it would go away.

Somehow I recovered and made it to the finish. Like a child, I had learned a lesson but also stretched myself and found that I was capable of achieving more than I thought. No doubt many others have experienced the same sense of achievement. The opportunities are there every weekend in this or any other area of activity for anyone who can be motivated to turn off the television, get up and out of the chair and take to the hills or the bike or the swimming bath or wherever an invigorating challenge is to be enjoyed.

The Long Distance Walkers Association puts on a 100 miles

cross-country event every year, and this was a challenge that Sandra couldn't resist. She thought about entering the 1981 'Cumbria Hundred' - but sense prevailed, as the thought of jogging around in the mist up Lake District peaks, probably getting lost and falling into a gully or down a cliff, convinced her to wait till the easier 1982 Pilgrims Hundred, in the south of England.

This 'easy' hundred miles just involved walking or running, or mixing it, from Guildford in Surrey to Canterbury, along the route taken by many pilgrims to the shrine of the murdered Thomas A'Becket. In fact there was a longer option of 140 miles, from Winchester via Guildford to Canterbury. Looking back on it, I'm rather surprised that Sandra didn't enter me for that one.

Navigating should not be too difficult on a path that essentially goes along the ridge of the Downs, all the way to Canterbury. If you found yourself slipping off to one side, then it was a fair chance that you had gone off-route.

But, of course, it's never quite as simple as that; and we did get lost a couple of times - if not too disastrously. Since I'm reasonably good at navigating, and actually turn the map the right way up - which is more than Sandra does! - we managed to make it across the River Medway, with the Norman castle and Rochester Cathedral on our left, to the breakfast stop at about 65 miles. We'd started at lunch-time, and it was indeed breakfast-time when we arrived, so we had taken it pretty leisurely.

Even so, I was absolutely 'all in'. Not so Sandra, she danced into the hall, fidgeted around with her spare clothes, and went to breakfast. She nattered away to everybody, put away her torch, got out the next lot of route-descriptions, and jumped up, ready to go!

I had just slumped into a chair, and remained there, staring at the cornflakes that I couldn't even summon the energy to eat. I made some feeble mutterings about her going on, and not to wait for me - and I might see her sometime in Canterbury. But, on the other hand, I might still be here, looking at my cornflakes the following day. So, with a cheery wave, off she went, and I remained in a stupor.

After about an hour, I eventually got through the cornflakes; and, as I was allowed an hour-and-a-half stop before being disqualified, I began to down a cooked breakfast and large mugs of tea, grabbed marmalade sandwiches like there was no tomorrow, and just made it out of the door, having decided that I might try to make it to at least the next check-point.

The trouble with leaving a check-point is that you get a bit disoriented, and sometimes fail to make the critical decision as to whether you should turn right or left out of the door. Well, needless to say, I turned left, went round in a circle, found the route-description didn't make much sense - and ended up back where I'd started.

As I wasn't allowed back in for another breakfast, I turned right and eventually made it to the next check-point, where I slumped down with some more tea and more sandwiches. After the maximum 15 minutes stop, I thought I'd make it to the next check-point. It was now around lunch-time and, with the sun up in the sky, I thought I'd have an ice-cream.

I met up with some other people who were going at a nice, sensible pace - and so, from one check-point to another, I eventually made it to Canterbury.

There was Sandra waiting for me - she'd showered, changed, toured the Cathedral, helped the people on the final check-point - goodness knows what else she'd done. But at least she'd heard that I had got myself going again, and so had stayed to give me a big hug.

Very slowly, we made it to the railway station, and then back to London. Then the frightening spectacle faced us, of actually getting out of the carriage and down onto the platform. We had completely seized-up and, as we opened the carriage door and looked down at this horrendous, precipitous drop - of about three feet! -we wondered however we were going to make it.

Eventually, I eased myself down backwards, Sandra passed down the rucksacks, and then I slowly helped her lever herself down onto the platform. We uttered great signs of relief, put our rucksacks on our backs - and then found we could hardly put one foot in front of the other to move along the platform. Looking rather ridiculous in athletic track-suits and impressive looking rucksacks, we were overtaken by old grannies, pulling their suitcases, or tapping along with their sticks at seemingly world record pace.

Of course, by the time we got home, had a long soak in the

bath, and slept like babes, the sense of challenge and achievement, and the sheer experience overwhelmed us ... well, at least it did for Sandra because, on the walk, she had heard about another 100 mile event, taking place later that year, under race walking conditions.

As far as I could make out this meant you had to walk at a cross between a penguin and a soldier. If you managed to complete this ordeal, which was to be on hard roads around the lanes of Leicestershire, then you could be elected to the 'brotherhood' - and presumably 'sisterhood' - of Centurions. The sheer name conjured up all sorts of Masonic connotations and mystery.

Walking like a penguin for a hundred miles, round and round in a circle seemed absolutely daft to me and I declined the invitation. But for Sandra, the challenge was too much. She had also heard about the first Centurion, John Fowler Dixon, who, like her, had also been a civil servant. He used to train by leaving his office in Whitehall at lunchtime, hailing a hansom cab -this was around the 1880s-1890s - telling the cabby to drive to Regent's Park. While he was doing that, he would change in the cab. When he arrived at Regent's Park, he'd tap the roof, tell the driver to stop, and get the horse to go at a gentle trot around the outer circle of the Park.

He would then walk between the wheels of the hansom cab. When he'd had enough, he'd shout to the driver to stop, get back into the cab and change while the horse trotted back to Whitehall. He'd pay the driver, return to his office, and get on with his work. Presumably he had an office to himself!

The other thing that probably drove Sandra was the fact that the sport had been dominated by men. She subsequently did some work to find out about a few female walkers who braved the roads and the prevailing dogma, to show that women could also compete in endurance events, like walking from London to Brighton.

Essentially athletics, and walking in particular, had been a male-dominated sport. It had been only a few years previously that Ann Sayer had blazed the trail for long-distance ladies' walking. She had refused to be told that she couldn't enter an event, and would just turn up. If they would refuse to issue her with a number, she would just walk, saying it was a public road or a public park - and that she could walk along it like anyone else. Since Ann is some six feet tall and weighs rather more than I do, perhaps the officials were reluctant to grapple with her, and to remove her forcibly from the event.

This was all good stuff as far as Sandra was concerned and so in August 1982, Sandra became 'Centurion 735' - that is, the 735th person to have walked 100 miles in under 24 hours, since records began at the end of the 19th Century. Her time was 22 hours 18 minutes.

After completing the Snowdonia 100 miles in May 1983 (running and walking across some marvellous scenery, and completing the 100 mile cross-country without getting seriously lost in the quite respectable time of 26 hours 29 minutes), I thought I would also have a go at the 100 mile event. In that year it was being organised by the Surrey Walking Club, which we had both now joined.

Sandra said that she would support me, because ladies were not allowed to enter the Surrey 100 mile event. Although she had completed the Leicester 100, Surrey was a very traditional club. It had admitted ladies only a few years earlier and some of the rearguard were certainly not going to set another precedent by allowing a lady to walk a hundred miles, particularly not around lonely lanes at night. All sorts of visions - or, perhaps, exciting fantasies - were conjured up of Sandra being assaulted in deepest Surrey's stock-broker belt in the middle of the night. Maybe they were just afraid that she would beat too many men from the Surrey and Stock Exchange clubs!

And so it was that I became Centurion 760, in a time of around 21½ hours.

Next year, 1984, saw us do the Dartmoor 100 mile cross-country around some marvellously bleak, open moorland, followed by the Leicester Hundred where I finished in 18 hours 50 minutes, and Sandra set a new British record of 18:36:29.
She really stormed the last few miles, and was only some seven minutes outside the world record for 100 miles, although at the time, she had no idea about world records and never thought they could be within her grasp.

That was in July. Only just over a month later, she won silver medals at the European Veterans' Games at Brighton - at the ripe old age of 35 - in both the 5km track and 10km road race walks. After the 10km on the Friday, we jumped on the train and went straight up to friends in Chorley, in Lancashire, arriving late that evening, to enter our first 24-hour running event.

After the sprints of the European Veteran Games, Sandra promptly set a new 'World Best' for 24 hours on a road surface - 131 miles 583 yds. It was quite remarkable to have gone from a European Championship silver medal for race walking 5000m on the track to a 'World 24 hours Best' for running on the road, both within 48 hours.

Not that the Chorley circuit was exactly ideal. It was in a park, and the tarmac was not particularly even. Indeed, tree roots broke through in various places, and one had to be careful not to trip up, especially in the middle of the night, as there were virtually no lights. It also had a slight hill in it, and there was at least one very sharp right-angled turn around a tennis court. So you couldn't swing out - you just had to do a 90-degree turn on the run.

In those days, we weren't very scientific about what we ate or drank; I remember that half-way through the event, just before the local fish-and-chip shop shut, our friends went out and brought back enormous bags of this traditional Lancashire fare, and we had a great slap-up meal.

I had developed a very swollen ankle, perhaps having twisted it on the tree-roots or at the right-angled turns and had to stop running and, eventually, to stop walking at 97 miles. I rested for quite a few hours and put cold sponges on, to try to get the swelling to go down; while Sandra - like some incredible running-and-walking machine - kept racing round the circuit, smiling as always at everybody.

Stan Jewell, the organiser, was getting increasingly excited and kept flicking through his record books to find what the World Record was for 24 hours. With an hour and a half to go, I got to my feet and, using an upturned broomstick as a crutch - with the brush-part underneath my armpit - I hobbled around for 90-minutes to complete 100 miles.

With Sandra's 131 miles added to my relatively feeble score, we won the team trophy - the first time that Surrey Walking Club had ever won a running trophy, and probably the first time a husband-and-wife team had ever won an ultra-event.

It was a marvellous moment as, in our own different ways, we had given it all we could. But the laurels, of course, went to

16

Sandra in her tremendous 24-hour debut.

So what lessons can be drawn from our early years in long distance running and walking?

First, it does not require great natural ability to be world class. You do not have to be acquiring swimming medals from your early teens to join the ranks of those that can enjoy the winning experience. If 30 year olds can crank themselves up to set records, then you can realise the potential within you. It is never too late to start.

Secondly, you do not know what you are capable of achieving until you try. So experiment. Do what gives you pleasure. Follow your instincts. As you push out your boundaries, so you surprise yourself. Then go that bit further. Set yourself stretching objectives. You do not know what can be achieved unless you have a go.

Thirdly, if your mind can embrace an objective, no matter how far off, or difficult, you will achieve it. If it requires a physical effort, your body will have no option but to follow where the mind has led it. It may hurt on the way, but if the mental will is there then with training and a steady build up of stamina the objective will be reached. If you or your organisation has the will and the commitment, you will achieve your objective.

Fourthly, it will be fun. Enjoy the adventure, smile on the way and the smile will be returned. It will help when things are a bit down. Since you never knew you were capable of achieving what is now being achieved, you are in a winning position. So relax and enjoy it and feel the warm glow excite you to still greater successes. You can't lose.

4

Know Then Thyself

"Know then thyself
Presume not God to scan.
The secret of mankind is man"

None of us know what we are capable of achieving. As a result we could set ourselves targets which are either too ambitious or not stretching enough. So we need to stand outside ourselves and in the cool light of day take a good look at the raw material we have to work with. We need to know ourselves. We have to be honest and set down our strengths and weaknesses. We should assess the environmental and other constraints within which we have to operate. We need in other words to do the type of analysis which any organisation has to do before it establishes its objectives and then sets off down the road to achieve its goals.

"A person is what his deep desire is." (Chandogya Upanishad)

It is not easy to be honest with ourselves and write a balanced assessment of strengths and weaknesses.

"There is no expedient to which a man will not resort to avoid the real labour of thinking." (Joshua Reynolds)

It is difficult enough for a company to be objective in its analysis. If anything, we all tend to underrate ourselves in good old British fashion. "No success please, we're British!".

But we have to do the analysis ourselves. As with a company, there is only so much help that others, like consultants, can give to do the job. The process of self analysis is as important as the end product. It forces us to be honest with ourselves, to shake off the baggage of assumptions, the layers of masks we have put on to protect ourselves or to project an image which is not our true self.

We have to peel off the layers, like peeling an onion, or removing the shell from a nut to reveal the shining chestnut which is our true self. Removing the sometimes discoloured and prickly outer layer is not always a pleasant process. Unwelcome memories

18

as well as joyous ones are recalled. Old sores are opened which we have plastered over. But as the layers fall away, we should feel relief that the facades don't have to be kept up any more. They can be seen as the inhibiting encumbrance they really are; a shell which has weighed us down and prevented us getting out, revealing and drawing strength from our true self.

I am reminded of the middle aged actor, who said what a great relief it was when he could be his true self and, recognising his age, not have artificially to draw in his flabby stomach and expand his hairy chest whenever he walked from his sunbed to the hotel swimming pool.

Boethius said: *"The perfect and divine source of happiness is possession of the true self."*

It may take weeks and many attempts before we feel we have really been honest and got down to our core self. The facades, the masks which we hide behind, the appearances and images which we try to keep up will be stuck like layers of paint. We will in many cases believe in the painted images we are presenting and act the part we have created, or which others have created for us.

"But if I strip myself down to the reality, how awful that would be. Just as I put on creams and mascara and lipstick and perfume to hide or improve myself, so these other images are necessary if I am to hide the real selfish, inadequate and weak me."

Is that really true? The Victorians went about "improving" churches. But in our generation we have come to appreciate "The Churches the Victorians forgot" (as one interesting book is entitled). Sometimes layers of sterile whitewash have been removed to reveal fine wallpaintings covered over by Puritans as well as Victorians.

In the last few years, we have even come to recognise the decorative works of the Victorians which were in turn sometimes hidden by later "improvers" or "refiners."

In music the search for authenticity has taken such a hold that Baroque orchestras playing on period style instruments with minimum vibrato seem to be springing up all the time. Authenticity has even reached the state when the Queen's Hall London Orchestra of the time of Elgar has been recreated using instruments of the time.

Getting at reality, trying to be authentic and seeing things as they are meant to be in their own terms of reference has come of age. Yet still we are loathe to accept ourselves and those around us for what we are. Maybe it is time we all came of age.

The Taittiriya Upanishad expounds the theory of the human being encased in five wrappings (like some Russian doll). Starting from the material body, (the first "self" of which we are generally aware), the writer takes us internally through vitality, mind, intuition and finally joy. As we go through the various levels or sheaths which cloak us, we experience quantum leaps of awareness. Even in the state of joy we grow until we become joy itself.

"The self in man and the sun are one.
Those who understand this see through the world
And go beyond the various sheaths of being
To realise the unity of life."
"When one realises the self, in whom
All life is one, changeless, nameless, formless,
Then one fears no more. Until we realise
The unity of life, we live in fear."

Partly our problem is one of conditioning. We have all been influenced by well meaning parents, teachers and friends who have made us aware of the dangers, the risks in life, of our mistakes and how we can do better. They have in the process bred in us a natural caution ("don't do that, you could hurt yourself"), a negative sapping of confidence ("I told you, you couldn't manage it; now look what you've done), an enfeebling attitude on trying out new things ("leave that to me, you're not strong/tall/quick enough") or even new ideas and approaches ("don't try and be clever"). What a dreadful remark that last one is! Our confidence and self belief can be undermined so easily and insidiously until we come to doubt our own capabilities.

"I am not yet born; oh fill me,
with strength against those who would freeze my
humanity, would dragoon me into a lethal automaton
Would make me a cog in a machine, a thing with
one face; a thing; and against all those
who would dissipate my entirety, would
blow me like thistledown hither and
thither or hither and thither
like water held in the

hands would spill me.
Let them not make me a stone, and let them not spill me;
Otherwise kill me. "
("Prayer before birth" Louise MacNeice)
We should rather apply to ourselves the thoughts of Pablo
Casals
"We should say to each (child): "Do you know what you are?
You are a marvel. You are unique. In all the world
there is no other child exactly like you.
In the millions of years that have past, there has
never been a child like you.
And look at your body ... what a wonder it is.
Your legs, your arms, your cunning fingers, the way
you move! You may become a Shakespeare, a Michelangelo,
a Beethoven. You have a capacity for anything.
Yes, you are a marvel .... "
("A world worthy of its children" Pablo Casals)

Recapturing the spirit and sense of achievement, of wonder and
of excitement is, I believe, fundamental to personal renewal. We
can do all the analysis imaginable and convince ourselves of the
need to take action, but if we don't rekindle that spark of
enthusiasm and excitement, we will not turn the potential into
reality.

Paralysis by analysis, reorganisation for reorganisation's sake
and as a substitute for creative innovation, are all diseases which
afflict those that need vision and resolve. We can "delayer" and
"re-engineer" an organisation until it becomes exhausted and so
lean and slim that it develops corporate anorexia. So often this
embracing of the latest management fad merely reflects a lack of
belief, of confidence and of determination to get out there and take
on the competition with enthusiasm and an eagerness to listen, learn
and innovate.

When Pru Leith, the celebrated caterer, became Chair of the
Royal Society of Arts, she put it admirably in the context of the
small and medium sized enterprise (SME):
"If it has the characteristics of youth - the potential and the
desire for growth or improvement or both, the flexibility of mind,
the eagerness for new ideas, the experimentation, responsiveness,
resilience and enthusiasm of youth - then that is my SME. I prefer

to call it the "eager" company, or the "ambitious" company."
(Quoted in FT October 1995).

As individuals and organisations we have to resist being pushed about or pushed under by the mass of conflicting pressures and signals we receive. We must not conform for conformity's sake when that leads to the denial of our true self and the frustration of our potential. We must not distort our goals to try and impress or please others. Everyone's task is unique and what absorbs us is a better guide to our true vocation than long lectures and yards of advice from others. We must be like the proverbial champagne cork which, when pushed under, bounds upwards on it's bubbles. We need enthusiasm and a zest for life; the "eagerness" and "ambition" Pru Leith so admired.

But what if we have lost that zest? What, for example if we are unemployed or facing redundancy? One of the effects of youth unemployment is that the experience of apparently being unwanted, of not having a useful role to perform, of being perceived as surplus to anyone's needs, can scar those individuals for life. Even at school, so many cannot see a worthwhile job let alone career at the end of their studies. Under such circumstances, how can motivation and incentive be maintained? How can belief in the self and our innate abilities be sustained? How can young people's energies be turned in a positive direction rather than either negatively to crime or apathetically to the TV?

There are no easy answers. But a positive self belief by individuals and support by others who have a mission to help others can achieve results.

In South Bristol a Canadian with just such a missionary zeal established the South Bristol Learning Network. John O'Hara took 50 unemployed young people and gave them basic hands-on training in computer skills. He and his small team, with some support primarily from ICL and the local TEC, helped those kids to "surf the Net," see the potential of modern communications, appreciate what information and opportunities were available. The enthusiasm and natural abilities for computer games was directed at increasing their computer literacy and numeracy.

Many of those young people got jobs in the growing telephone/computer based industry of direct financial services or the expanding BT directory enquiries/freephone service. Others moved

22

into smaller companies.

Within 18 months, over 1,000 people of all ages and backgrounds had been through the basic Cyberskills course. The schools in South Bristol were then connected electronically and linked with the local Further Education College, the library and Enterprise Agency in a broadband local area network suitable for life long learning with interactive voice, text and video.

This area, which had been desolated when Hanson moved in and closed down the major employer, (Wills Tobacco, following the takeover of the Imperial Group), has become one of the greatest test beds worldwide of local community-based regeneration, reskilling and life long learning. Its lessons are now being emulated elsewhere. Who would have thought of starting such a high tech experiment with a bunch of unemployed kids in a run down unemployment blackspot? John O'Hara had the vision and by sheer belief and perseverance turned it into reality.

"People are always blaming their circumstances for what they are. I don't believe in circumstances. The people who get on in this world are the people who get up and look for the circumstances they want; and if they can't find them, they make them. " (Bernard Shaw)

The same is true of market leaders in so many sectors. They re-write the rules of the marketplace, re-define and set new customer needs and standards. They don't just satisfy customer expectations, they exceed them and produce delighted customers who will return again. I didn't know I needed a Walkman until Sony sold me one...now I would not be without it on multi-day events.

Looking for the positive opportunities and then going for them with vigour and enthusiasm distinguishes the successful from the ordinary. It marks out the achiever from the doubter who only looks for reasons why something can't be done.

If we think positively and look for opportunities, then our actions will be similarly motivated. Our minds condition our actions. If we develop our minds in a positive direction and draw positively from first experiences, then we will feed ourselves the basis for a similarly purposeful future.

It is all too easy to look backwards and think negatively of weaknesses, deficiencies and excuses. The negative can even come to dominate our thinking and paralyse our actions. How often, for example, do we revive those embarrassing moments from the past as though they had occurred yesterday? How often do we go over again and again the experiences of failure or how we might have said or done things differently? How often do we wish we had some of our time again?

It is one thing to learn from the past and put those lessons into practice in the present and the future. It is another thing for the past to dominate and consume us, sapping our confidence and preventing us from charting a new course. Success is an attitude of mind, a journey that we are continually embarked on, continually learning, continually looking forward to the next experience.

"It's a funny thing about life, if you refuse to accept anything but the best, you very often get it." (W.Somerset Maugham)

It is not easy to get that sense of balance between learning from the past, learning in the present and putting all those lessons into action to achieve positive results. As athletes, for example, we have rightly been shown videos of ourselves and compared our styles with videos of the world's best. But in pointing out technical deficiencies and developing a programme to focus on them, it is all too easy to ignore the strong points, the features that have brought success and which may give us the edge over others. It is particularly easy to undermine the confidence of young athletes, who inevitably have technical deficiencies but nevertheless have that all important spark of enthusiasm and desire to improve and to have fun.

A rigorous training schedule aimed at achieving world class standards should be balanced with other sessions which are more relaxing, more varied and fun to carry out. There are many different ways of achieving the same result. No schedule must become a grind or motivation will be lost and the vital spark extinguished.

When I was out in Odessa in the Ukraine towards the end of 1995, taking part in a 24 hour run, young enthusiasts of 9 and 10 years of age were throwing shot puts with both hands in front of them on the track and then chasing after them. They would throw them again and again to see who could be the first to reach the end of the 100 metres straight on the track. They were developing their shoulder and arm muscles in a way which gave them fun. Their shot puts knocked into one another like a game of giant marbles or

24

boule and the air was filled with their excited laughter.

In athletics, and any other area of life, we also need to recognise the individuality of the athlete. The analysis and assessment of physical factors from cardiovascular fitness, to power to weight ratios in various muscle groups and the resulting programmes of endurance training, weight sessions etc need to be devised creatively and in ways where improvements can be recorded and thus progress demonstrated.

Throughout our early years in long distance walking, we always tried to maintain a sense of balance so that our lives did not become completely consumed by the sport. Maybe that partly reflected an innate caution or lack of belief in our true potential. But whether by design or not, the mixture of hard quality training for speed and strength, more relaxing all day hill walking for stamina, and weight/gym sessions for muscle development, kept our interest while securing continuous, measurable progress. I hope it was also a reasonably professional approach which reflected our own needs and which suited us.

I would suggest that a sporting self awareness checklist also needs to cover environmental and external factors which are likely to affect performance in such a way that problems have solutions. External factors such as school or college exams, pressures from family and friends, financial problems, long travel times to training sessions, even the timing of menstruation against key dates for competition all need to be handled both systematically but also sympathetically. Finally the analysis of attitude needs to unearth what can inhibit a performance such as pre-race nerves, lack of mental focus, fear of the opposition or fear of pushing oneself through self imposed mental barriers. Whatever the analysis produces, we then need specific resulting plans of action and mental training. I will return to this in a later chapter.

In our analysis, planning and training we must, however, never extinguish the spark which inspires. It is this which drives the greatest sports people to their greatest achievements.

Seb Coe had great technical ability, but it was his inner will which grasped the gold medal for the 1500 metres at the Los Angelos Olympics in 1984 after his earlier defeat at 800 metres. Sally Gunnell's hurdling technique was second to none when she won Olympic, World Championship, European and Commonwealth gold medals, but no one would doubt her fighting spirit.

25

Being positive with a zest for living life to the full is the fundamental difference between a winner and an "also ran", whether that is in sport or any other area of life.

The positive approach can sometimes take us by surprise and shake us out of a set way of thinking:

"Some people are always grumbling that roses have thorns; I am thankful that thorns have roses. " (Sara Teasdale)

Success is built on having this positive attitude of mind. We need to believe we can reach out and touch it. Practising and perfecting what we want will help us build confidence and self belief. We can achieve anything which our inner mind can embrace.

We can then think positively and can create a list of strengths and achievements.

We can write down our answers to such questions as:

What was the achievement that gave me the greatest pleasure?

Why was this?

What is the best thing people say about me?

What would I want to be remembered for?

What have I yet to achieve that I would like to do?

What is holding me back?

How can I overcome or get round any constraint?

When can I start?

Why not now?

(For a fuller list of suggested questions, do look at "The Eureka Principle" by Colin Turner).

When people have been made redundant, they can feel their world has collapsed. They feel they are entirely to blame. They are all too aware of their weaknesses, how they could have done things better, how their relationships with other could have been better handled. They tend to forget their achievements, the part they played in growing or supporting a business or just keeping the show on the road, the friendships built up, support offered, customers, suppliers or staff pleased by particular actions or words. They forget the specific plus points which when written down can built up an impressive record.

Everyone should draw up an asset register of themselves. Just as companies set down their assets either on a Balance Sheet or increasingly off balance sheet where peoples' skills and brand images are concerned, so individuals should have their own asset register listing the qualities they possess and bring to their current or future job or to areas and organisations outside of work. An example is on the next page.

This is for someone that has perhaps been in the retail business as a sales manager and is now thinking, or having to think, of what other jobs that person might do. The list on the left-hand side shows the skills and experience that has been acquired and that could be brought to various jobs. The row along the top is possible jobs.

The last column headed "Director of a Charity" may seem like a wild card. But actually the analysis suggests that the person has many of the skills needed and that on a simple scoring calculation, the qualifications are well suited. After a hectic and pressurised job as a sales manager, the fulfilling - though equally frustrating and hardworking - post of a charity director should at least be seriously considered.

The analysis helps identify not only our attributes, but also the future both within and outside the work environment which best suit us. We can score the qualities needed for a particular job to help determine what best matches the skills we have. In the example opposite, a score of three means the skill is highly relevant for one particular job, while a score of one suggests it is hardly necessary.

It is important to be both honest and rigorous in the assessment. It is no good having unrealistic aspirations and wishing for the moon. I remember the lovely radio advert for the Royal Mail Recorded Delivery Service. Against the background noises of cows and in a broad Somerset accent, a person laments that his application for a new job had not been received. *"And I were looking forward t' bein' an astronaut"* he said!

Realism and an absence of self delusion is important. There is no point in drawing up a wish list which is totally unrealistic and unachievable. That will only produce disillusionment.

The asset register is important whatever our ambitions. It will help systematise and rationalise the inner sense of why one activity seems naturally to be preferred over another. Following our

PERSONAL ASSET REGISTER

EXPERIENCE/SKILLS	SALES DIRECTOR	MARKETING DIRECTOR	COMMERCIAL DIRECTOR	GENERAL MANAGER (MD)	DIRECTOR OF A CHARITY	
1 Retail Industry	3	3	2	2	2	12
2 Technical Knowledge	3	2	2	2	1	10
3 Marketing Skills	3	3	1	2	3	12
4 Market Research	1	3	1	1	2	8
5 Conference Organisation	3	3	2	1	3	12
6 Strategic Planning	1	3	3	3	3	13
7 Sales Skills	3	2	2	1	2	10
8 Profit Responsibility	3	2	3	3	3	14
9 Management Skills	3	2	2	3	3	13
10 Teambuilding/Motivation	3	3	2	2	3	13
11 Product Development	1	2	2	2	2	9
12 Legislation and Licensing	1	1	3	2	1	8
13 International Operations	1	2	3	2	1	9
14 Charity Fundraiser	2	2	1	1	3	9
15						
16						
17						
18						
19						
20						
	31	33	29	27	32	

Rating: 3 Highly Relevant   2 Relevant   1 Useful

instinct is important; but an analysis of why our instincts are telling us something and leading us in a particular direction is also necessary, especially when options present themselves and a rational as well as emotional response is needed. We can all delude ourselves if we are not careful as to how nice it would be to escape and be a crofter, sail around the world or take the marketing job just falling vacant. Hence the systematic approach via a carefully drawn up asset register will help us in the search for building on our real strengths.

If we have done the job properly, then we will be more aware of ourselves, of our current limitations but also of our potential. Self knowledge produces self confidence. We are all better than we think and have greater potential than we realise. Self doubt is a great crippler. The aim of analysis should be to help us overcome our self doubts, accentuate the positive, believe in it and prepare ourselves to act upon it.

From greater self awareness, comes greater self confidence and belief.

In the early church, one of the greatest theologians was Gregory of Nyssa. He wrote a treatise called "The Life of Moses" on that orphaned, initially stammering and nervous person who became one of the greatest leaders in history.

When he comes to talk about the burning bush and how Moses had to take off his sandals he says:

"Sandalled feet cannot ascend that height where the light of truth is seen. Equally the dead and earthly covering of skins, which were placed around our nature when we were found naked because of disobedience to the divine will, must be removed."

Moses takes off his shoes as if his false self is being removed. His untrue self is left behind and his true self sees, hears and responds to what has been waiting for him. Moses comes face to face with the person he really was as he faces the burning bush, the real burning mission which was to engulf him.

Of course he is terrified at what he sees and hears. He knows that what is being asked of him will engage him in the use of enormous and frightening power. He tries to wriggle and make excuses "Who shall I tell them sent me?" "How shall I speak?"

"Isn't there somebody else?"

He struggles, he squirms, but he knows he has come face to face with his mission in life. From then on he finds he is free. At first he is given Aaron to hold his hand and speak for him. But soon he is making his own speeches and does not need Aaron. Once he has accepted his own inner calling, he grows in confidence and strength.

"Each one of us is involved in the same journey as Moses. We are all involved in a struggle between our false and true selves. We have to come face to face with our own burning bush. We have to see it within our lives and obey its call."
(Melvyn Mathews)

We are also involved in a struggle against a Pharaoh. Psychologically speaking, he is the tyrannical ego-self, the great "I am." We have to do battle with this tyrant and set the children of our true self free. We have to live our lives out of the burning bush, hidden as it is deep within ourselves.

Like Moses, this is a frightening experience because we have to accept total responsibility for our lives based on our own beliefs. It is often easier to live comfortable lives looking after someone else's sheep down in old Gidian! It is easier just to follow the safe paths, to let others take responsibility, take the risk, take the blame if something goes wrong.

"Moses is the exemplar of the self maturing into freedom; the freedom that allowed him to come face to face with his God and his true self and whose freedom then released others. The children of Israel symbolise all that is locked away in ourselves, all that needs to be set free. In the end, only coming face to face with the God within us will release those children into the Promised Land."

Really know yourself. Take the time and be honest in your self assessment, what you really want to do in your life, where your inner self would really want to take you. Construct a full check list and establish your own asset register. From greater self awareness comes a plan of campaign to remedy deficiencies and realise the potential you have now revealed.

Self knowledge removes self doubt and hence provides the basis for soundly based self confidence and a realistic plan of campaign.

Being positive and having an unshakeable determination founded on inner belief are the ingredients that separate the exceptional achievers from the ordinary, the winners from those that drift with the tide.

"What we are today comes from our thoughts of yesterday; our present thoughts build our life of tomorrow; our life is the creation of our mind." (Buddha)

5

Setting the Vision

"Without vision the people perish" the Bible says in Proverbs 29.
Seneca used a suitable aphorism for a Greek trading nation: *"No wind is a fair wind when you don't know what port you're aiming for."*

Any person who aspires to unlock and achieve his or her potential must set a long term goal. The vision for the world class athlete might be:

"Winning a medal at the Olympics in five years time."

The goal must be stretching but also realistic. It must be long term but not so distant that it cannot be seen or reached in measurable steps. Neither must it be so vague that you do not know when you have got there. It must not be some fudge under which you deceive yourself as well as others. If you cannot touch it, measure it or quantify it, then I suggest it is too vague.

I like to think of it as an Italian city set in the Tuscan hills. It may shimmer in the heat and be unfocused as you look towards it, but it is a definite, tangible objective and you will know when you have got there. Not all the path may be clear and there may even be some options but the overall direction must be unambiguous.

For the Forrest Gump run our vision was simple: *"Set new records for running from Land's End to John O'Groats."*

A vision for a business or organisation is no different. It also has to have substance, something that can be quantified and measured. Notions such as:

"The best oil company in the 1990s"

beg more questions than they answer.

Admittedly, for an organisation the audience for the vision statement will to some extent affect its content. Vision statements serve external as well as internal needs. For the individual on the other hand, the vision will often be private, or at least for a limited audience.

For an organisation, the statement indicates to the outside world the high ground the company wants to reach, or in John Harvey-Jones's words *"A better picture of a better tomorrow."* It will signal to shareholders why they should continue to invest for the long term; to customers, employees, suppliers and the wider community how the organisation will position itself not just to satisfy their needs but also, hopefully, to delight and excite them. "Satisfied customers" may be good enough for the average business but not for the best that must offer that bit more.

If it is to meet these needs, then the vision statement needs to be simple, easily comprehended and something that people feel they can live with.

The "Statement of Purpose" from British Gas which dropped through my letterbox in 1992 was, I feel, one of the better statements I have seen.

"We aim to be a world class energy company and the leading international gas business."

Today, their adverts on Classic FM radio still pick up those twin themes of a world class energy company and the leading international gas business. Whatever else British Gas may have got wrong in its public relations, its central vision certainly appears to have been well founded and has withstood the test of time. It is also simple and easily understood. At the same time, it is stretching ("the" leading international gas business at a time when the company was only just starting to develop its international interests) and flexible (viz its reference to a world class "energy" company) which leaves open the potential for diversification into non-gas business areas. The reference to "world class" also implies knowledge of the competition through benchmarking and the aim to be amongst the best in the world.

The statement is also interesting in that it makes no reference to profitability. This is surely right. Profitability is the result of having a stretching but realistic vision for the long term, of having delighted customers who recognise that the organisation provides exceptional value and something extra which others do not provide and which perhaps they were not expecting. A hotel which provides as a matter of course fresh flowers in the room and a bowl of fruit and a drawing or picture book at meal table for a young child might be examples which are still too rare. At little cost however they provide that something extra.

How are the best visions created? Who sets the route map and decides which city on the hill is the goal?

In sport, the sportsperson has to set the goal. He or she has to believe in it, understand the implications, the dedication that will be needed, the changes that have to be made and what will have to be given up in the single-minded pursuit of that goal. It will be a more personal, more private statement than an organisation's mission statement.

But even the athlete does not set the vision alone. If he or she has a coach, then the decision will be taken jointly after much consultation. Others will also be involved. The athlete's family will need to own the goal. There will be sacrifices that they will have to make. Friends and training partners, school or college teachers and friends and many others will need to buy in to the long term objective and the shorter term implications.

If the sporting vision is a team's vision such as:

"Winning the world football/rugby/hockey cup in five years time"

then clearly the numbers that have to buy into that vision are increased considerably.

Even so, someone has to create the vision.

Will Carling has described how Geoff Cooke, the England Rugby Union Manager presented his vision of England reaching the 1991 World Cup Final to the National Squad in 1988 in a hotel room. He later admits that "reaching the final" was an inadequate vision because it did not imply the single-mindedness of purpose which would have come from the notion of "winning the World Cup." Even so, at the time this was a somewhat startling announcement since England were far from a successful side. The vision thus meets the criteria of not only being simple and easily communicated but also stretching and just achievable.

It was also the vision of one man. Someone has to have the inspiration and the inspirational leadership to drive towards the goal set.

The same is true in any organisation. I do not believe that visions emerge from committees. Consensus, commitment and hence wider involvement are certainly vital if the goal is to have any chance of being attained. Many organisations fail to achieve that consensus of purpose. The vision is just despatched from on high to come thudding down on the desk of the poor front line salesman who has to carry it out. But despite the need for wider ownership of the vision, someone has to light the fire and hold the torch aloft in the first place.

In the military field, Montgomery took over a demoralised Eighth Army in North Africa and inspired it with a new sense of team mission, a belief that it could win. In politics, whatever one thinks of Mrs Thatcher, she had a sense of mission which changed the course of British political and economic life; and when she focused General Galtieri in her sights, he and everyone else knew it!

If the leader has to have the vision (and no-one can profess to being a leader without having a vision) he has to communicate it and secure ownership of that vision if the organisation is to be motivated to getting there. Grand statements of intent which have no substance in reality are not worth the banners they are written on.

Although vision setting is essentially top-down, I suggested above the importance of an organisation buying into that vision. Indeed, provided the leader is part of his team and not divorced from it, the vision will not have sprung ready formed from his breast. It will reflect the leader's own experience, discussions and input from those with whom he is in contact (and especially the Board). The more widespread the involvement and consultation, the more the likelihood that it will be firmly based.

The process of creating and testing the vision will bind the top team together and make them think through such fundamental questions as: what business is the organisation really in, what should it be in, where ideally would the top team like it to be and what role do the various business units (which might be subsidiary companies) have to play in achieving that vision. Such searching questioning may throw out some fairly fundamental and even unpalatable issues on what role a particular subsidiary has to play (is it "core" or not) and on the role of the corporate centre.

For any group should only exist in its particular form if it can better add value to its collection of subsidiary companies than any other group. The process of developing the vision statement will

35

identify the source of that added value, the type of culture and control systems that are implied (the Strategies and Styles so well identified by Goold and Campbell) and should ensure that this added value is enshrined as the basis for future expansion.

Lord Sheppard, Chairman of Grand Met concluded an article on the development of long term strategy as follows:

"The investment of time and resources in the process of developing a corporate vision and long term strategy for Grand Metropolitan has proved to be a major motivator and integrating force throughout the Group. It has channelled the energy of our managers who strive towards their highest aspirations. It has positioned us to exploit strategic opportunities much more efficiently and quickly in the future. Finally, but not least, it has caused us to build and enhance the strategic capability of the corporate centre."

And what about the individual?

Within an organisation, we must develop our own mission and jointly those of the team of which we are a part. This must be related to the wider organisation's mission. Developing a coherent and consistent set of obligations requires a bottom-up as well as a top-down approach. It is, after all, on individual and team performance supported by motivation that the performance of the wider group depends. How many organisations talk about "people being our greatest asset", but then do precious little to harness that asset and release the untapped potential that exists in every team and individual.

To develop our mission in an organisation we also must have a wider vision to which we aspire in life. The purpose of going through our self analysis, identifying our strengths, weaknesses and opportunities, and establishing our personal asset register, is to enable us to renew ourselves through a personal mission statement.

All organisations should encourage every member of their teams to develop personal mission statements and to see how they can best be aligned to the missions of the team. Only that way is it possible to release the potential of individuals within a team, enabling job satisfaction and overall productivity to increase.

Through such a process an organisation can work to discover the hidden assets and overlooked ideas and opportunities that exist within itself. It can also set about aligning the aspirations of individuals with those of the team. If the setting of the vision cannot involve everyone and has to come from above, the alignment of top-down vision with bottom-up personal objective setting has to take place if individuals are to know and feel how they are part of and can best contribute to the wider group objectives.

At a time of continuous change and uncertainty, it is important that every individual has training and support in thinking through their own objectives, how their strengths can be recognised and developed and their own careers progressed so that job satisfaction and productivity are maximised.

As I note later on, there is at last a broad realisation that *"individuals are now the only source of competitive advantage"* (CBI) *"Investment in education and training is, in principle, the best investment available to individuals, companies and nations."* (RSA)

The essential factors in business transformation are not only such features as:
- clearly defined missions, values and a clear sense of what provides a company with its competitive advantage;
- fast response times in meeting changing customer needs;
- lean manufacturing with a partnership approach to suppliers and all other stakeholders;
- the application of technology and the creation of a culture which encourages both innovation and an ability to listen and learn from external and internal ideas.

Transformation also requires renewing the spirit of the workforce, encouraging a partnership where they can contribute, can do something ennobling and responsible (not just work), and develop their own potential both within and outside the work environment.

Because no organisation can guarantee a job for life, employees should be offered another form of security through being trained to develop a clear and realistic view of how they wish to develop as individuals. Being equipped for an ever changing environment, knowing what skills and strengths people have and being motivated constantly to seek self renewal through life-long learning is the way to greater self reliance, a feeling of self security and ultimately self fulfilment.

We all need to boost our desire to know ourselves, develop our own plans, increase our desire to learn and take advantage of the tremendous opportunities which modern technologies are making available to us for distance learning at our place of work, in our homes, our libraries and in groups as well as at more traditional centres of learning such as schools and colleges.

It may be that the self analysis and setting of personal missions reveals that the individual is in the wrong job and could contribute more in another role. It may be the missions of the individual and organisation are not compatible, in which case an early parting will save frustration, low morale and low productivity. The process and subsequent mentoring may however enable the person's aspirations to be developed through additional training, support for evening classes or through being given responsibilities and encouragement in areas outside of the immediate work environment.

This wider perspective is I believe important. We tend to compartmentalise our life into for example work, family life, sports, social, gardening etc. etc. But it is the same person carrying out these roles. We cannot simply divide ourselves or pretend what we do in one area of activity can be divorced from how we perform in another area.

If we feel invigorated from a day in the hills or inspired by a book we are reading or a concert we have been to, then we will take that additional motivation into work. If we have had a row with our partner or the kids, then we will take that into work. If we have something to look forward to at the end of the working day, then we are likely to be more positive and more invigorated than if we are only going to be a couch potato falling asleep in front of the television.

It is interesting that the British Olympic Association, in its scheme Planning for Success, confronts the motivational aspects and the need to balance sporting commitment with the rest of life. *"It is not strictly a time balance, but a matter of becoming a whole person,"* says the BOA technical department. *"You must not forget that there is more to life out there."*

A BOA psychologist has speculated that one reason behind Jennifer Capriati's fall from grace as a young superstar tennis player may have been that she could not cope with all the mounting pressures, financial, parental, coaching concerns. The conclusion that emerges from US and UK work in this area is the need to maintain a balance between the sporting and non sporting life.

That's also useful for when a career has passed its peak. *"A lot of athletes don't realise they have developed some very good life skills in their sport. They forget this when it comes to using them in real life."* It is scary sometimes to go into new areas where you do not think you have much experience. In fact people have more experience and capabilities than they realise if they have developed a more rounded approach.

Maybe we still have an attitude of mind which has been conditioned by the so called "American system" of manufacture with large firms and mass production, in which everyone is allotted a specific function. This compartmentalisation influences our approach to work and to life in general.

It is surely time to change this. The founder of one of the worlds largest electronics companies, Konosuke Matshushita of Panasonic, put it starkly and simply when addressing a Western audience:

"We will win and you will lose. You cannot do anything about it because your failure is an internal disease ... You firmly believe that sound management means executives on the one side and workers on the others. On the one side are men who think and on the other side are men who can only work. For you management is the art of smoothly transferring the executive's idea to the workers' hands.

We (in Japan) have passed this stage. We are aware that business has become terribly complex. Survival is very uncertain in an environment filled with risk, the unexpected, and competition ... We know that the intelligence of a few technocrats - even very bright ones - has become totally inadequate to face these challenges. Only the intellects of all employees can permit a company to live with the ups and downs and the requirements of the new environment ... It is why (Japan's) large companies give their employees three or four times more training than (those in the UK). This is why they foster within the firm such extensive exchange and communication."

If we believe, Konosuke Matsushita, tapping the aspirations and abilities of individuals within an organisation is not just desirable but vital for future survival.

Until recently, we in the West have been too dismissive and even ignorant of the Eastern approach to business and to life in general. We have much to learn from the more holistic approach which has for long characterised Far Eastern society.

We should drop the division between labour and leisure, following instead the Confucian adage that

"the master in the art of living makes little distinction between his work and his play. He simply pursues his vision of excellence in whatever he does."

The chairman of the major Korean company Samsung is clearly well imbued with this philosophy. He has summarised the outlook he would like his corporation to take:

"By balancing our work life with our personal life, we will achieve increased performance and productivity."

Hence, his corporation decided that employees should start work at 7.30 am so that they can finish work in good time and pursue and be supported and encouraged to pursue personal developments in sport, music, the arts or in other areas - including as part of a family grouping. They are actively encouraged to spend more time with the family and to sustain the development of family values. Some politicians and businessmen in the Uk are wondering whether there is not a lesson there for our society.

There is admittedly in Korea an inner tension between the hierarchical, paternal approach to business and employees and the desire to free the initiative of individuals so they can contribute more to the success of the corporation in the ways that Konosuke Matsushita was suggesting. But the attempt to create a better balance within an individual's life, thereby helping that person better fulfil his or her potential is genuine. The founder of Samsung (the father of the current Chairman) said that:

"The Samsung employee will be a leader of the people, greatly contributing to the happiness of mankind."

Such a holistic objective is unlikely to feature in many UK companies' Mission Statements.

He also said that the model Samsung employee is *"A person who possesses a creative, ambitious and dedicated character."* Would you find that as the HR mission of many major western companies? In their search for cost competitiveness they have sometimes lost that creative spark, that ambitious streak which inspires the dedication of those who want to be associated with success.

Would that some western companies had the same corporate philosophy as Samsung;

"We apply our human resources and technology to create quality product and services and thereby contribute to society. "

Do we see "our nation as a deep rooted tree" with "culture as a stream flowing from a deep well" which we should all dip into and is freely available to all? As we slump in front of our TVs watching American or East London sitcom pulp, I wonder. When we think of achievements in the West, let us remember that the world's earliest printed book, the Dharani Sutra had been produced in Korea before AD751 when we in the UK had kicked out the Romans and were running around in the Dark Ages.

Samsung has said that it will be one of the top ten corporations in the world in terms of sales by the year 2000 and one of the top three firms in electronics. Their mission is clear; their commitment unambiguous; they are tapping and fostering the skills and strengths of their workforce and I suspect they will achieve their mission.

It is not too late for western companies to emulate the approach of Eastern Tigers. Competitiveness is not (with respect to Peters) at the level of the country; or even at the level of a specific industrial sector such as aerospace or machine tools; it is at the level of the company. There is no inevitability about a company's success or failure; it depends on management's attitudes, on their flexibility and willingness to learn, adapt, meet and ideally anticipate and even set future customer standards and aspirations and tap creativity and unused potential that exists in every organisation.

Encouraging individuals to assess their own potential, to give them the opportunity to direct their creativity and energies as a positive force in line with wider group objectives is central to corporate renewal. The opportunity to excel in whatever they do in life and wherever their talents take them are objectives which must be surely at the heart of every organisation. A more holistic Eastern approach to business and personal needs seems increasingly appropriate.

Interestingly, the 1995 UK Institute of Personal Development

Conference in Harrogate moved some way to the East with the recognition that an essential factor in successful business transformation is *"renewing the spirit of people - appealing to their desire to do something that is ennobling rather than just work."* *"We need to give people something they can believe in."*

As one speaker said, there is a need" to create a forum in which the wisdom of ordinary people deep down in the organisation can be heard and focused into company strategy."

"You can't renew a company without revitalising its people." (Prof Ghoshal, London Business School)

Maybe if the 1980s and early 1990s were the decade of finance, quick returns (and quick collapses!) then the rest of the '90s and the first decade of the new century may indeed see a focus on the development of people.

"Individuals are now the only source of sustainable competitive advantage." (CBI)

Some of the forward-looking statements of Anita Roddick, the founder of the Body Shop reflect these themes and some of the thoughts in this book:

"You have to look at leadership through the eyes of the followers and you have to live the message. What I have learned is that people become motivated when you guide them to the source of their own power and when you make heroes out of employees who personify what you want to see in the organisation."

"You educate people, especially young people, by stirring their passions. So you take every opportunity to grab the imagination of your employees. You get them to feel they are doing something important, that they are not a lone voice, that they are the most powerful and potent people on the planet." (Quoted in Topics Issue 3 1995)

The Body Shop's Mission Statement has an even greater sense of mission than that of Samsung:

"To dedicate our business to the pursuit of social and environmental change;

To creatively balance the financial and human needs of our stakeholders;

To courageously ensure that our business is ecologically sustainable;

To meaningfully contribute to local, national and international communities in which we trade by adopting a code of conduct which ensures care, honesty, fairness and respect;

To passionately campaign for the protection of the environment and human and civil rights and against animal testing;

To tirelessly work to narrow the gap between principle and practice, while making fun, passion and care part of our daily lives. "

What powerful statements of belief to back up Ms Roddick's passionate belief in her staff and their mission!

Would that more companies had the passion, the enthusiasm, the eagerness of youth displayed here. Would that more supported the excellence and development of their employees in areas outside of the narrowly perceived work environment. Too few see the benefits for staff motivation, for productivity, for creativity and hence ultimately for business success which comes from a more inspirational and holistic approach to life and work.

Achieving this approach is, however, not easy. It may mean compromising in many areas so as to achieve a preferred overall balance. This may even mean that excellence itself is compromised. It may be difficult to achieve excellence in athletics, at work and as a family person all at the same time. It may well be impossible. Excellence requires such commitment that it's pursuit can become all consuming. It can be like a drug. The athlete cannot do without two or three training sessions a day. The worker wants to work all night. The family man wants to be home early to give his family his undivided attention. The three are in conflict. Something has to give. Or does it? Is it compromising or achieving a more satisfying and ultimately more rewarding and sustainable balance and perspective?

Sandra and I have tried but maybe not entirely succeeded in achieving an ideal balance between all the different pressures and opportunities which face us. We have, perhaps managed to be world class athletes despite, rather than because, of the culture and environment in which we live. The same must be true of so many people. For us it has meant training at 6.30 am before work and then after work wherever we can. Our lives have revolved around a restricted pattern in which theatres, restaurants, concerts and other activities have taken not even a back seat. To be world class really requires a focus and dedication which few are willing or able to give.

Does that mean that the pursuit of excellence cannot be fully achieved? In terms of the single minded development of one attribute that may be true. But would such a total single mindedness of purpose make us better people? Would we be happier? How long could we have sustained it? The pressures to perform and "triumph" (in the eyes of the outside world) would have been immense; (just look at the pressures on Linford Christie or other top sportsperson); and would the fun, the exhilaration, the vital spark have been lost? And what about our daughter; what happiness and what personal development would she have achieved if both parents had been focused solely on athletic excellence?

"The purpose of human life is the pursuit of happiness." (American Declaration of Independence)

Happiness comes from personal fulfilment. We have achieved satisfaction and hopefully received and given pleasure in the process. We have developed our potential as far as we could within the boundaries of a reasonably balanced and sustainable life. We have gone on and continue to go on enjoying developing and fulfilling our potential when many others would have burnt out.

Although we probably cannot aspire to achieve the visions set in the Upanishads, we can at least have that vision of a balanced, united perfection before us:

"Where one realises the indivisible unity of life, sees nothing else, hears nothing else, knows nothing else, that is the Infinite. Where one sees separateness, hears separateness, knows separateness, that is the finite. The Infinite is beyond death, but the finite cannot escape death." (Chandoya Upanishad)

Let us return to the vision which we have each set ourselves, shimmering on the hill ahead. A route is now needed to get there, a route with useful pointers and markers recording progress. (Not like the lost walker who stumbles to a crossroads in the night, sees a white post with pointers on it, but when he shines his torch only illuminates the words "wet paint!").

We need some useful intermediate milestones and the best way to set these is to work back from the vision.

Establishing milestones will also help assess the realism of the vision. If they represent a credible and necessary progression, they will highlight what has to be achieved over the coming months. If that looks unattainable, then the vision will have to be changed or the timescale for its attainment put back. Going through the process of setting intermediate objectives will thus provide an important test of the longer term vision.

The nearer the objectives become so the more numerous they are likely to be. You can see the route toward the distant hills fairly clearly over the immediate few hundred yards and hence can more easily judge what has to be achieved. There should always be a natural progression and a logical relationship between the various milestones. They should also remain as tangible and quantifiable as possible. As you move along the road, you should be able to tick off the milestones as you pass them and know exactly what you have to do to get to the next one. So for the athlete to reach the vision of "winning a medal at the Olympics in 5 years time," may require him or her winning the UK Championship in 3 years time, getting into the British team in 1 years time, setting a personal best time and inning the area championship in 6 months time.

Exactly the same process of setting milestones is needed for any organisation. The company aiming for market leadership in a particular product or market sector will need to have realistic milestones. How otherwise can it and its various stakeholders have confidence that it will reach the chosen objective? The milestone might only be achievable as a result of a takeover or radical increase in marketing expenditure. Hence, milestones drive the setting of the accompanying strategies.

The organisation aiming to double its membership over five years (say youth club or a church) will also need to have intermediate objectives. This is particularly important if the support of sponsors is in any way conditional on progress down the chosen path. The organisation will need to show it is on track and thus can fulfil its side of the bargain.

The milestones Sandra and I set for the Land's End to John O'Groats run were a mixture of athletic and planning objectives.

On the athletic front they were:
- successfully complete at least one 200Km race walk in the previous 12 months;
- defend our UK 100 mile walking titles in respectable times;
- complete a 6 day race 6 months before LE JOG (Sandra had

never undertaken such an event and I needed to try out different rest patterns).

- complete at least two 25 mile cross country runs 3-4 months before LE JOG followed by a 50Km walk 2 months before and a 200Km walk 1 month before; these would build up stamina.

On the planning front, the milestones were fairly basic:

- find a team manager;
- put together 2 teams;
- secure significant sponsorship;
- finalise a start date.

A whole host of other items on the critical path would then have to be addressed; but without these four the show would never get on the road.

With clear objectives, we now had something to aim for, something to excite and inspire us. Something that will get us out in all weathers, down the gym when it opens before dawn and committed to go that bit further in training.

"You must have great willpower in an event" someone once said to me. "Yes" I responded, "But even more willpower to train."

In an event, the adrenaline is going and the thrill of the race takes over. On a cold, rainy winter's day there is no such joy. But it is the quality of training which will determine the subsequent performance. Commitment during training is just as important as determination in a race. It has to be there all the time, in all seasons and in all places.

Before we consider the subject of commitment, of "wanting" something, and of being determined to achieve it, let us summarise some key points.

The positive spark which will light your whole being with enthusiasm and drive is enshrined in your vision of your future. It is the light on the hill ahead which draws you inexorably on. The vision may be an individual's or that of a crusading team. But to be achievable it has to be owned and have the commitment of all those on whom its realisation depends.

The route towards it is set by clearly identifiable and quantifiable milestones.

The milestones will establish what you have to do next year, next month, even next week to achieve the vision. If you cannot meet next week's milestone, then go back to the vision and be realistic about what you can achieve.

Achievement needs a commitment to life long learning. The learning sessions should be like fresh water springs along the road. We must continually renew ourselves if we and our organisations are to be equipped to meet the rapidly changing future.

Test the vision on those that also have to buy into it if it is to be achieved. We will see later that it is thanks to a team effort that we achieve our own Everests.

We must not however think of the vision on the hill as an end in itself. It is part of a process through which we aspire to still higher and greater awareness and realisation of ourselves. As such it is an endless process.

6

Winning with the Mind

In the 1952 Helsinki Olympic Games, Emile Zatopek of Czechoslovakia made history by winning a unique treble of gold medals in the 5,000 metres, 10,000 metres and marathon. He was totally self motivated, reportedly training in combat boots and full dress and going out to run across the snow until he collapsed. He washed the family clothes by jogging up and down on them in a wash tub. His fanaticism was matched by the pained expression on his face and he obviously knew how to push himself through repeated pain barriers in training and competition. We can never know exactly what motivates such people to achieve sporting excellence but an over-riding desire to achieve for whatever reason is absolutely crucial.

When Zbeigniev Klapa, the great Polish ultra distance walker, was asked why he thought Roger Quemener had won the 335 mile Paris - Colmar race for a record seven times while he had come second, he responded, *"I guess he was prepared to accept more pain than I was."* The next year, Klapa started a series of wins in this gruelling race across half of France.

Chris Bonnington in his rivetting compendium "Quest for Adventure," cannot at the end of the day easily explain a person's inner drive, and the extremes to which he and fellow adventurers are prepared to push themselves in pursuits that have no direct material benefit to themselves or mankind in general. He concludes that the events are creative entities in their own right deriving from inner willpower. Looking at the background of the adventurers described in his book, they came from all walks of life, some from unhappy homes, some from well integrated families, and in all shapes and sizes. Physical and environmental characteristics and backgrounds appear to have been of less importance than inner drive in the achievement of success.

How is that inner drive created? Is it just a question of you either having it or not having it (as some would have us believe); or it is possible that you can develop and enhance your willpower through mental training? Can that inner desire be directed so as to become not just brute ambition but something more joyful and ultimately more satisfying and meaningful; something which embraces all of life so that our creative energy and drive become part of something greater?

On a wall in our London flat I have a picture of Daley Thompson winning Gold at the European Championships. It is the end of the final event, the 1500 metres. The track is littered with the bodies of his competitors. Daley stands exhausted, alone but supreme amongst the debris. When asked why he hadn't collapsed as well, he responded in typical Daley fashion, that he would have done if there had been room for him to lie down!

It was Daley who said:

"The only limitations are mental; you can do anything you want, and the guy who thinks most positively will win."

We should all say that every morning when we get out of bed, before we start a race or take on any major task.

David Hemery (that great Olympic hurdler) expressed similar thoughts when he said: *"Our mind is the key to achievement. Our thoughts, whether conscious or unconscious determine our action."*

We are all conditioned by our thoughts which reflect the influences we have absorbed in life. We are all to varying degrees brainwashed and programmed from an early age to respond in certain ways. Sometimes those pressures are all to the good. They may help us to think of others and how our activities or words may affect them. Our social skills, our concern for those less fortunate than ourselves, our awareness of our environment and of the damage and waste we can sometimes inadvertently create are all reinforced by external influences.

But so too are our doubts about whether we really can achieve something great or unique, whether we can push out the boundaries of our own experience and experiment by launching ourselves into unknown territory. Conformity, accepting, playing safe, not risking anything, not rocking the boat, are so often the pressures we feel.

At school the emphasis remains on "learning" rather than

"creating." The innovative lateral thinking child is thought of as a disruptive influence who can't focus on the task in hand. An attitude of mind is bred which produces excellent analysts, problem solvers and managers but precious few entrepreneurs, innovators and risk takers. The more far sighted recognise this as a major weakness in the UK at the current time. But little is done to incubate the spirit of adventure and risk taking which marked us out in previous centuries. We suffer from too many administrators and bureaucrats who have been trained to be reactive, risk averse, being "a safe pair of hands."

The negative attitude, cynical approach, sarcastic remark is so often preferred to the constructive, the creative, the positive. Maybe this reflects a basic insecurity. Maybe as a country we are still uncertain of our way in the world post Empire with our ambivalent attitude to the rest of Europe and our love-hate relationship with the USA. Maybe it is a reflection of our not yet having come to terms with the ending of job security, the job-for-life company which could safely nestle so many families almost from cradle to grave.

Where are the venture capital funds that invest only in those entrepreneurs who have failed on the basis that they will have learnt so much from their failure but yet still have the urge to risk all in the pursuit of their ideas? Such funds exist in the seething cauldron of innovation known as Silicon Valley in California.

Where is the university which tries to attract students with the slogan *"Come to us and become a millionaire."* For so many the thought of grubbying their hands with the real live commercial applications of their research work remains anathema. Research attracts the researcher. The go-ahead innovator goes elsewhere - often to Silicon Valley.

We are in danger of losing that sense of personal initiative and freedom which has distinguished us from the more centralist bureaucracies and regimes in Central and Easter Europe for example.

As we take on responsibilities for a family, a mortgage, our retirement, so the loss of individuality and personal initiative can increase. Even an evening out, making the effort to create entertainment and involve others can lose its appeal and the enemy of initiative, the TV, gives us our thrills at one remove. We start to vegetate. We waste our potential without even realising we had any. We start to die mentally and physically before our time.

It may require more effort to be constructive, innovative and positive. We have not been conditioned in that way. Criticising is easy. It makes us feel superior. But we must recognise that such a destructive, negative attitude gets us nowhere. Being negative is the mark of a mediocre mind.

The great steps forward were taken by leaps of the imagination, by the creative mind, by those that were excited by looking at old problems in new ways. The jet engine would never have been created by someone trying to perfect the steam engine. The steam engine would not have come from someone perfecting the stage coach.

We can all unearth potential if we so choose. We can all think positively. As children we were terribly creative and imaginative with pieces of wood, stones, water, anything that was to hand. We can shake off the layers of heavy clothing which have burdened us ever since and think how we can again derive and give pleasure and satisfaction often from simple things, often from helping others. We can all derive a sense of achievement as a result.

Thinking positively is not a zero-sum game. There is not a limited amount of positive thinking in the world. It does not have to be shared out. Rather the reverse. The more of it there is around, the more it will take hold and excite everyone around us. Like a fire it will spread and change us.

The fire analogy has strong associations. We have already seen how Moses was brought face to face with his future at the burning bush. He had to take off and leave behind his assumptions and previous self, just as he had to leave behind his sandals. When

"The angel Gabriel from Heaven came
His wings as drifted snow
His eyes (were) as flame"

to make the great announcement to Mary that she would be the mother of Christ. Similarly, when John the Baptist announced that someone greater than he was coming, he also used the fire analogy, *"He will baptise you with the Holy Spirit and with fire."* That fire would sweep away fear and cleanse from the inside making us aware of the truth that is within all of us.

Maybe the positive, winning frame of mind needs a health

warning:

"A positive frame of mind can seriously improve your achievement in life. It is addictive and highly contagious." As you exhibit symptoms, others will also catch it. As a result we could all be changed.

Opposite the picture of Daley Thompson in our bedroom is a cupboard where I hang my shirts. Inside this cupboard door I pinned the poster advertising the 1989 330 mile Paris-Colmar race. The poster showed the route and a large central picture of the contestants from the year before. I also pinned there some photographs I had taken of some of those contestants climbing the hardest section of the route over the 3300 ft Col du Bonhomme, which comes right towards the end of the race before the final descent into Colmar.

Every morning, when I came to put on my shirt, I would open the cupboard door, and there would be the great challenge facing me with the people I would encounter. Every morning the challenge was encouraging me to get out and train.

The route slowly became engrained on my mind until it held no fears. I may not have walked it, but my mind had come to terms with it. I knew each town and how far they were apart. I realised where the hills were. I had marched up the Col du Bonhomme a couple of hundred times with those walkers in the photographs.

When it came to my turn to stand at the starting line in Paris, in the summer of 1990, I knew what I had to do. My mind understood and my limbs seemed to have caught the right spirit and were prepared to drop into the right gear right from the start.

Of course there were problems on the way. The feet began to fall apart. I ran out of energy a few times through not eating and drinking enough and through my crews not forcing me to refuel when I became incapable of deciding for myself. By the finish, I was sleepwalking and hallucinating and had to be prevented from staggering to the right or the left by having crew members walking either side and giving me a gentle push back on course if I started to walk into the ditch.

But at no time was there ever any question of not making it. My whole body and mind had been conditioned over the months to think only of the map which had a start point and a finish. On the climb up the Col, we just walked as in the picture at a steady pace and as I had imagined it so many times. There was nothing daunting about the Col. I had climbed it so often before in my imagination.

The vast majority of contestants do not complete the gruelling Paris-Colmar at their first attempt. For some it takes many years before they finally make it. Some never make it. I am sure that the mental preparation was a major factor in my successful assault at the first attempt. I became only the second British walker ever in the history of the race since it started in 1926 to cover the complete distance within the time allowed. The other walker was Colin Young, who completed it as the Paris-Strasbourg in the early 1970s. Colin was delighted to return as a key member of Sandra's support crew as she became the first British woman to cover the distance. We were the first ever husband and wife couple to complete in the history of the event.

That poster and the photographs are still pinned behind the cupboard door. They now serve as a reminder not only of that great race, which Sandra and I have also subsequently completed, but more generally of our achievements. If ever I were to question my capabilities, the inside of that cupboard door should remove any doubts.

When I set my earlier Lands End to John O'Groats running record in September 1988, I was utterly convinced that we would be successful. I only booked the vans for the time it would take to get down to Lands End, complete the 830 miles in under 11 days (the record was then 12 days 1 hour) and return to London. The times for meeting supporters at such places as Chorley, Preston, the Lake District and Edinburgh, and for crew changes at Bristol and Warrington were all planned on the basis of a record-breaking schedule.

There were times when it was hard work and extremely painful but that just meant we took a bit longer. My mind never had any doubt that we would set a new record.

The same was true in 1995. The feet might complain, but the mind has to tell the body to get on with the job in hand: *"You knew it would hurt; and you volunteered for this; no one has forced you to do it; it is your choice; this is what you have been training for, building for and you know you are going to make it in record time; so just get on with it."* As a certain advert says *"Just do it. "*

At no time on the Forrest Gump Run did either of us even contemplate not getting to John O'Groats. Such a negative thought never entered our minds.

There were times when Sandra was in such distress, especially with her feet but also partly with her stomach, that her crews suggested they pack it in. "We have gone over 400 miles. That's tremendous. But look at your feet. We've still got another 400 miles to go. Be sensible."

Sandra's response was very quietly and deliberately to put on her sandals (her feet were so bad that she could not by now wear her trainers), slowly get to her feet and say quite calmly, *"I'm going for a little walk. Would anyone care to join me?"*

Humbled and silenced in the presence of this awesome display of utterly focused commitment, Sandra's team fell in behind and began themselves to believe they would make it, to be fully committed to the unique exploit they were undertaking. They would follow her all the way or until their leave ran out.

Even one tough member of Sandra's crew who knows what it is to go through the valley of death and come out the other side had said, *"If you were my lass, I would put you in yer sleeping bag and take you home."* When Sandra reached John O'Groats, he was there, having himself walked several hundred miles with her. For mile after mile he would be a couple of yards in front so she could focus on the back of his reflective jacket and be drawn along. His commitment became total.

As Sandra got back on the road, she repeated one of our favourite motivational phrases. It summarises our belief in what sorts out the achievers from the rest of the pack: *"When the going gets tough, the tough get going!"*

Just repeating that phrase gives you a sense of determination. It makes you believe in the remarkable capabilities which we all have if only we care to draw on them.

The phrases become mantras which you repeat over and over again. They almost hypnotise you. They certainly help you focus and relieve some of the pressures which can sap confidence or make you lose focus.

For no matter how confident someone might be, no matter how well the training has been going, as a major event approaches, some nervous tension inevitably builds up. It has been estimated that about 80% of the time sports people spend acquiring psychological skills revolves around coping with pre-race nerves and with associated relaxation techniques. No doubt the same is true of anyone about to put him or herself to the test especially if there are others looking on.

Sometimes the pressures result in an individual being plagued by persistent negative thoughts. If we focus on our pains and discomforts, the symptoms somehow become more exaggerated. I have heard how opera singers become neurotic at the slightest cold or tickle in the throat. Some athletes can become convinced that the competition is unbeatable just because they have not beaten them before. Alternatively, they can become stage struck and almost in a trance. Did this happen to Seb Coe in the Los Angeles Olympics 800 metres?

Derek Underwood, a rugby international, saw the benefits of mental training as follows:

"It helps me calm my nerves before a game with relaxation techniques. And during the game there is positive thinking so that if you do make a mistake, however trivial, it doesn't play on your mind; you're going to be able to shut it away and get on with the game."

The same needs exist in a business or in any organisation. A loss of nerve, a focusing on the risks rather than the opportunities, a lack of commitment at the vital moment to drive forward and grasp the prize, can result in that organisation's potential not being realised.

If the analysis has been carried out rigorously and even ruthlessly, if as a result a vision has been agreed which is stretching but also realistic, and if the milestone steps along the way have been marked out, that should give confidence. But there can still be a failure of nerve. That often means a failure on the part of a few individuals.

A business can succeed with a faulty plan if the drive and commitment from the whole organisation is there to make that plan happen. Without that drive, and a search for constant improvement, all the planning is wasted. It is motivation that secures action.

In any area of life, those who believe they can't are right;

those who believe they can are also right. "Can" and can't" become self fulfilling prophecies. *"Can't is a four letter word."*

If we can recognise and articulate the tensions and pressures upon us, we are half way to removing them. We can then face them and see if they are shadows or have substance. So often it is the fear of the unknown which holds us back.

Sometimes we just have to step aside and allow the pressures to subside. Perhaps a period of relaxed detachment will provide new vigour. Short term pressures can then be removed and the strategic essentials brought back into focus. Board away days are marvellous for reinvigorating the top team in a business. Quiet days at a retreat provide spiritual renewal. A mountain training camp revitalises an athletics squad.

Relaxation techniques are also an important part of reestablishing equilibrium and reinvigoration. They can involve progressive muscle relaxation (eg: from the neck and shoulders down through the whole body), localised relaxation in specific muscle groupings, deep and slow breathing and many other exercises. Some border on yoga while others, which I perform, involve a regular pattern of warm up, exercise drills and even a routine of slowly changing into sports gear, dressing feet and applying lotions. Because of its familiarity, the routine helps to make me feel at ease, to focus into myself rather than on the external hurly burly and remind myself that I have done all this before and been successful and it is just a question of going out and doing it again. Such techniques also help on long airline flights and even midway through a hectic business schedule.

Warming up, stretching and checking all the working parts at racing pace can also help in the build-up of final pre-race confidence. Slow, deep breathing not only aids the feeling of calm, but also energises the mind. The expansion of the chest and stomach seems to fill the whole body with air until the muscles constrain the expansion and give back a feeling of confident power. This can be reinforced by the repetition of positive thoughts such as *"I am in great form," "I am strong and fit," "Today I am unbeatable," "My inner power will lead me on."*

Visions and complex feelings can be reduced to a single word which encapsulates the positive approach needed to win. This word can be repeated and the whole body focused on its implications.

56

The word might be "power" or "float" or "glide," the latter to emphasise the effortless quality which can epitomise the greatest athlete. Words associated with relaxation rather than tension and gritted teeth can take you above and beyond the competition, almost in a mystical sense. Sri Chinmoy has a marvellous description of the Spiritual Forces running life's race with us. The Spirit does not run so far ahead that it leaves us behind. It is only just in front, tempting us just to reach out that little bit further and touch it and thereby gain refreshment.

Those that have developed the techniques of yoga and reciting mantras have an advantage. But there is no reason why anyone should not latch on to a word or short phrase and use it to focus the mind on the key tasks ahead.

Focusing by a single word or phrase can be supplemented by visualisation. Many sports people visualise themselves surging past competitors. Positive race results become embedded in the mind. Others kick a rugby ball to convert a try from all angles of the pitch and in all conditions and all imaginable external pressures, so that it becomes second nature.

I remember reading Sally Gunnell's description of how months before a major event (be it Olympics, World Cup or European Championships) she would start visualising the final. She would imagine racing from lane 1 with its tight bend or lane 6 with its longer bend; the likely competition would be in various lanes for various visualisations; she would race in the boiling sun or pouring rain, or into a head wind in the final straight; every conceivable permutation was covered, so that on race day that race had already been run in the mind. There would be no reasons for surprises, uncertainties or misgivings and nothing would have been left to chance.

Visualisation can also apply to technique. Watching videos of top performers can give you a mental picture of how a champion performs. If this is ingrained it can be reproduced. In a long event when technique can start to fall apart, the ability to think about relaxation and the fluid style of champions and to be able to draw on that ingrained moving image can help hold everything together and minimise the wastage of effort which can come from a disintegrating style.

Visualisation is also important in areas outside of sport. Before any public speaking engagement, whether to a conference of a couple of hundred or an after dinner toast to a couple of dozen, it is worth not only seeing the venue, but also imagining yourself there giving the speech.

If you really have ambitions to be a great salesman or the next chair of the PCC or social club, then you should act out the part, "walk the talk" and feel at ease in that new role. You will be more convincing and stand a far greater chance of bringing about your objective.

An actor has to visualize and act out his part in the mind many times before he can comfortably walk into the new role. We all have to feel comfortable in the role we intend for ourselves. If it does not feel natural after some practice then maybe we will have to reassess whether we are being true to ourselves or not.

We have to ease ourselves naturally into new, winning positions and visualization is a form of training which can help us achieve this.

If through practice we can get it right, the results can transform us. In his book "Golf My Way" Jack Nicklaus says:

"I never hit a shot, not even in practice, without having a very sharp, in-focus picture of it in my head. It's like a colour movie. First I 'see' the ball where I want it to finish, nice and white and sitting up high on bright green grass. Then the scene quickly changes and I 'see' the ball going there: its path, trajectory and shape, even its behaviour on landing. Then there is a sort of fade-out, and the next scene shows me making the kind of swing that will turn the previous images into reality."

David Hemmery remembers when he set a new world record while winning the Olympic gold medal in 1968 at the Mexico City 400m hurdles:

"Only a couple of times in my life have I felt in such condition that my mind and body worked as one. This was one of those times. My limbs reacted as my mind was thinking: total control, which resulted in absolute freedom. Instead of forcing and working my legs, they responded with the speed and in the motions that were being asked of them."

For Ayrton Senna practising in 1988 for the Monaco Grand Prix the fusion was even more intense:

"I felt as though I was driving in a tunnel... The whole circuit became a tunnel... I had reached such a high level of concentration that it was as if the car and I had become one. Together we were

at the maximum. I was giving the car everything and vice-versa... Suddenly it was as though I woke up and noticed that I had somehow been on a different level of consciousness. I was really shocked and I went straight back to the pits - and didn't drive any more that day. I realised I had been in a kind of unending spiral. Faster and faster, closer and closer to perfection. But also more vulnerable. "

One is reminded again of the unity of life propounded in the Upanishads (perhaps prophetically reminded given Ayrton Senna's tragic death):

"One who meditates upon and realises the self discovers that everything in the cosmos - energy and space, fire and water, name and form, birth and death, mind and will, word and deed, mantram and meditation - all come from the self.

The self is one, though it appears to be many. Those who meditate upon the self and realise the self go beyond decay and death, beyond separateness and sorrow. They see the self in everyone and obtain all things." (Chandogya)

Two other mental training techniques are worth mentioning. "Association" is when an athlete focuses his mind entirely on the race in hand while "dissociation" is when the mind wanders or is diverted onto other matters. Both have their place.

I am often asked what I think about during an ultra event. The answer, "All sorts of things." At the start, my concentration may be on style, on sending signals around the body to check what is happening, checking if I am relaxed, monitoring my speed and elapsed time every circuit and over intermediate distances, working out times in my mind, thinking of tactics, checking on the intake of food and drink. Later on, the mind might take in the scenery or, as often in training sessions, wander freely over past races, or on problems which can be resolved when they are put in perspective. So many problems and tensions fade when placed in a wider, longer term context.

Later still in the race, it may be important to re-focus on style, on what has to be done to achieve the objective set and overcoming physical discomfort. If you are practised in the art of yoga and can really let your mind go into a beautiful state of peace, then you can ascend into the higher mental realms.

We can all to some degree reach a state of relaxed tranquillity. This often comes from a mixture of effort expended, the tensions of everyday life left behind and a coming to terms with the day and everyone and everything around you. Then you can feel the inner smile and the sensation of just floating along with a sense of oneness with all around you.

Sometimes in our races, when tiredness sets in perhaps just before dawn when the mind begins to drift and needs some stimulation or something to focus on, a Walkman with a suitably rousing tape can be a help. Sandra has been known to go for hours with one tape playing the Beachboys, Elvis or Kings College, Cambridge (Sandra has a catholic taste!). The mind can then turn away from thinking of tiredness, blisters or other problems. The only danger is that any such stimulus can lead to a burst of inspirational pace which feels great at the time but can destroy the careful balance of energy use and matched energy intake based on an even pace, which I am sure produces the best results.

Life is like a long distance event. If you charge off in a race you will soon slow, maybe "hit the wall" when you run out of energy or, worst of all, not finish the course. You must disregard those around you who tempt you to go faster than your natural pace, who induce tensions in you as they jockey for position. You must run your own race at your own pace.

So it is in life. If we charge off with manic tension, striving to achieve everything at once, we will either have to slow down or burn up. The tensions which threaten us prove not to be so very important in the grand scheme of things when we place them in a longer term perspective and view them over a lifetime.

We may stumble and graze our knees a few times in life as in the race, but we will pick ourselves up and continue if we have that steady inner burning desire to finish the race. We will help others who will go through difficult patches, and others will help us. We will make friends on the road and receive friendly waves and support and give back a wave, even when we are tired. Finally, we will look back with satisfaction and hopefully feel we have done just about all we could have done and no doubt better than we and some others might have thought when we started.

An event, like life, can also be split into stages. I always split long events into bite-sized pieces and work at each segment to a prearranged plan. For an event such as the Lands End to John O'Groats, you just have to think of one stage at a time, otherwise the challenge would literally not be comprehensible - the mind

60

cannot cope with thinking of going 830 miles. It can however cope with a five mile section to the next village. It can contemplate a 15 minute run followed by a 45 minute walk as part of a morning section to a 12 o'clock lunch stop. The mind does not have to try and comprehend even a whole day. It just has to focus on the next few miles and go from breakfast to lunch like it does on any other day of the week.

To help it over difficult patches, little rewards can be built in. "Fifteen more minutes and you can have some favourite bit of food"; "Just get to the top of this hill and you can have a long drink;" "You can soon run down the other side and that will put you well up on your schedule." And so the mind is coaxed along the road until it forgets its problems, its tiredness, any negative thoughts it had. It can then relax, come to terms with each stage and so be at one with the whole adventure.

Building rewards into everyday tasks can have the same positive effects. Waiting for a cup of coffee till you have finished a report will be more satisfying than breaking off mid-way. Promising yourself a beer or a favourite video if you complete the gardening or car repair will work wonders for the task in hand and enhance the enjoyment of the reward.

Many of the techniques mentioned above are relevant for individuals in any walk of life. Relaxation techniques are important whether you are in childbirth, or tense and frustrated in meetings or at the end of a hot day. A problem can become soluble if it is broken down into bite sized pieces. Visualisation is important for anyone who aspires. If you can think positively and visualise yourself in your future role, confidence will increase.

We are not impassive, non participating witnesses of our own life story. As in certain modern novels, there are a variety of possible endings. It is for us to chose. We have the ability to shape our lives, to create opportunities and place ourselves in those new positions. We can determine our own destiny.

Let us summarise:

Analysing ourselves, perceiving our capabilities and setting a clear vision in front of us will not automatically bring a positive result. We have to want that result.

The trouble is that we have been conditioned to play safe while finding it easier to conform, be cynical about new initiatives and criticise the creative. We are in danger of losing the ability to be innovative, entrepreneurial achievers in life.

But both positive and negative are attitudes of mind. If we can change our pattern of thinking and accentuate the positive and the possible, we can change our responses and our actions and hence our lives. The way we think determines the way we live.

To a degree we either have the right mental approach or we don't. But we can all search deep within ourselves and refind it. There is also a lot we can do to develop and focus it.

Visualisation will help us think ourselves into a positive future. Relaxation techniques can be supplemented by association and dissociation. We can focus on a single word or phrase which encapsulates our commitment to drive forward to our goal. Tasks can be broken down into bite sized pieces and hence a seemingly daunting objective can be made comprehensible in a step by step approach.

The worldly outer race, is however only part of a search for self fulfilment, part of an inner race. That race will have been won when we can fully come to terms with the result, whatever that might be, accept the oneness of life and our place in it and feel the serenity which comes from giving in joy of all that we are capable and receiving joy as we run life's race to the full.

7

Planning the Adventure

In 1989, Don Ritchie captured my 1988 Lands End to John O'Groats record by taking under 3 hours off my time of 10 days 18 hours. I wrote to congratulate him, but added that I hoped he would enjoy the record he was just borrowing. I had every intention of recapturing it.

That proved to be easier said than done. The Lands End to John O'Groats requires the planning appropriate to any major adventure. It means gathering together two van crews with three or four people in each that are prepared to give up time and perhaps even pay to come and support. It means finding the funds for the hiring of two vans plus petrol, food, drink, the cost of getting people to and from a main rendezvous point, as well as the cost of other equipment that will be needed such as mobile phones. Almost certainly, it means having to recruit and pay for one person with medical experience. The 1988 event had shown how vital it was to have someone that had physiotherapy and a broad range of general medical skills, and our subsequent races in France had also shown that you could not skimp in this area. Neither could you expect such a skilled person to give up time and hence loss of earnings just for the sheer fun and experience.

If, of course, Sandra decided to have a go at the ladies' record, then that would double up the costs and more than double the difficulty of raising an experienced crew, since we would then be seeking not just eight but sixteen "volunteers". It would be vital that we had a core of people that had experience of similar expeditions or multi-day events.

Undertaking the Lands End to John O'Groats also would mean a lot of running training. Increasingly, I was concentrating on race-walking and attempting first to win, and then to defend my National 100 mile title and then to have a go at the 100 mile and

200 kilometre UK records. There were also Continental Internationals to go for. Being selected for the British team, being British number one and hence the person on whom the team relies to gain as many points as possible through being at the front of the field, meant that every season became increasingly focused on peaking for one or two events. There was little chance of diversifying and entering running races.

Running and walking use two different sets of muscles. In walking you push off from the toes with a straight leg and use the hamstring muscles, calves and shins. To get the extra stride you will also swivel the hips. In running you will have bent legs and use the quadriceps and calf muscles.

The use of the two different muscle groupings has its advantages. If you can keep alternating between running and walking, hopefully you can give one set of muscles a rest while you are using the others. So long as you do not run until you grind to a halt and wear out the running muscles, you should be able to keep going longer and further than if you were just a walker or just a runner.

Malcolm Campbell, the president and effective founder of the International Association of Ultrarunners, expounded this theory to us over his gin and tonic (or two) in a Grantham pub when we were first getting into long distance eventing. Indeed it was the thought that we might be able to mix the two together when we were not at the time great shakes at either running or walking, which gave us some additional confidence to have a go.

Perhaps our concentration on race walking in the early 1990's and our successful completion of the gruelling 330 mile Paris-Colmar race walk from the centre of Paris to the German border town of Colmar, south of Strasbourg, proved a blessing in disguise. It gave us the experience of multi day events in a point-to-point race where you were always accompanied by vans and a 3/4 person support crew. It gave us knowledge of the type of food and drink our bodies not only needed but were also prepared to accept after hours and hours on the road. It gave us experience of sleep deprivation and of long hours in all weathers. Most important it gave us a hard core of seasoned veterans who, for some reason or other, were willing to turn out and put themselves through all sorts of discomfort. Maybe they are drawn by the camaraderie, the wonderful atmosphere that gets old ladies out in the middle of the night in their dressing-gowns and curlers, and children along the roadside to cheer you on as you pass through small ancient French villages. Maybe it is the waves from Frenchmen in their archetypal berets, drinking their coffee and brandy by the roadside. Perhaps it is the mini Tour de France atmosphere and the great feeling of exhilaration the whole team gets as you climb over the Vosges mountains with their spectacular views before descending the last 20 miles through cobbled Kaiserburg (oh how those cobbles are a torture for feet which have long since been rubbed raw) to the flowers and bands and cheers in the timber framed border town of Colmar.

Whatever their motivation, without such an experienced team and without their commitment we could never even have thought of mounting a serious assault of the Lands End to John O'Groats records.

Sandra and I had first seriously thought about a Lands End to John O'Groats in late 1993. We had already decided that the three Paris-Colmar events we had completed now needed to be followed by a different challenge. However we never really managed to get the planning organised for an event for 1994 and instead chose to enter a 6 day race near Sacramento in California. This was to be Sandra's first exposure to an event of such length and again it provided valuable experience.

6 day events have a long and honourable pedigree. In the eighteenth and early nineteenth centuries, letters were delivered from one estate to another by servants on horseback or on foot. In the days when even turnpike roads were often not much better than mud tracks in winter, the footmen became proficient athletes walking and running prodigious distances.

Slowly such feats were turned into races, as one lord would challenge another that his man could go further or faster than the other's. The result was a mixture of point to point races, such as between Birmingham and London or Bath and London (both about 100 miles) and events in one location, such as at Blackheath and Newmarket.

In May 1809, Capt Robert Barclay walked 1000 miles in 1000 hours for 1000 guineas on Blackheath. Having to walk 1 mile every hour and hence having to do without any long period of rest was as much part of the challenge as the actual distance which had to be covered.

Many others emulated this feat and women also entered this and other challenges. The prize money was after all substantial for the time. Bets also became large and fortunes could be won or lost on the result. Hence all sorts of shady practices emerged. Drinks were laced, roughs were hired to intimidate the pedestrian, they were tripped and jostled. The spectators grew in numbers and drunken brawls broke out. The weather was not always reliable either.

Writs to prevent the events continuing on the Sabbath were taken out for various reasons, sometimes by people who had bet on the wrong person and had a lot to lose. Not walking on the Sabbath was a good pretext for interfering with the course of a race. This soon had the effect of focusing multi-day events into 6 days. The race would normally start around midnight on Sunday and end late on Saturday - ie: 6 days.

Many were held indoors and by the 1870s most major centres of population had their stadiums where such events could take place. The greatest venue was the Agricultural Hall in Islington - the structure still exists. In the days before football, horseracing or athletics were organised spectator sports, these 6 day races attracted thousands of spectators. Side shows, bands and other entertainments were laid on, as well of course as food and drink.

Gambling was also allowed and large bets were made. The shady practices continued.

One of the great promoters of such 6 day pedestrian events was Sir John Astley. The Astley belt became a coveted prize and the holder was effectively the world champion.

When the belt went to the USA in the 1870s, Sir John encouraged a Mr Charles Rowell to train hard and then paid for him to travel to Madison Square Gardens, New York, to win it back. Rowell duly brought back the belt, having won with 500 miles. He also brought back £5,000 "a pretty good haul for a man who had seldom had two sovereigns to rub against each other."

Sir John Astley recalls: *"It was wonderful what interest the public took in these long distance performances. Hundreds of people came in just to have a peep and were so fascinated that they stayed for hours, returning day after day.... The money taken at the doors nearly always exceeded the prizes and expenses; so after giving away more than I advertised, I put by the surplus."* Ostensibly this was for a prize fund for walking and running different distances; but Sir John was also an astute businessman like so many promoters of today.

The distance travelled in 6 days slowly built up until Hazael reached 600 miles in New York in February 1882. Finally, George Littlewood recorded 623¾ miles in December 1888. That record stood for nearly 100 years. It was only in 1985 that the Greek runner Yainnis Kouros bettered it with 625 miles. It remains the British record.

I cannot resist noting the exploits of a namesake of mine "Blower Brown" who was helped by one John Smith. Sir John Astley describes "this peculiar brickmaker" in his book "Fifty years of my Life" published in 1895 and kindly drawn to my attention by Peter Lovesey, whose crime book Wobble to Death is set in the context of a 6 day race and is compulsive reading.

"Brown had early distinguished himself by the rapid manner he trundled his barrow of bricks to the kiln, and back again for another load, and, like all brick-makers (I have ever heard of), he was wonderfully fond of beer: therefore, when old Jack Smith wished to get an extra spurt out of his protegé, he used to yell at him on the track, and the same exhortation and promise was enumerated whenever his instinct told him encouragement was needed: 'Well done, Blower! go it, Blower! you have got 'em all beat, my beauty! Yes! Blower shall have a barrel of beer all to himself if he wins; go it, Blower!'

*One day Blower showed signs of shutting up, and as he was more an animal than an angel, Smith and I agreed that it would be a good thing to wake him up a bit by putting him in a hot bath - quite a new sensation for him - so we took him to my lodgings hard by, and I ordered two chops to be got ready for him, and then put him into a hip bath of **real hot** water, which livened him up considerably, fairly making him sing out. When we had got him nicely dried, the chops appeared, and whilst I was helping Blower into his running suit I was horrified to observe old Smith busily employed gobbling up all the best parts of the chops, leaving only the bone, gristle, and fat. When I expostulated with him on his greediness and cruelty to his man, he replied: 'Bless yer, Colonel!*

Blower has never had the chance of eating the inside, he likes the outside,' and, sure enough, the brick-maker cleaned up the dish, with the result that he won first prize, doing 542 miles, a grand performance, and, what is more, his appetite and thirst were in no way impaired."

That was in April 1879.

As to the benefits or otherwise of long distance races, Sir John has no doubts:

"One word re the utility or otherwise of these feats of endurance. My opinion is, first, that any means by which an honest penny is to be acquired by those who need it ought to be encouraged; secondly, that it is good for man to know how short a time for sleep or rest in the twenty-four hours is really essential to sustain the physical powers of his body; thirdly, that it is quite as good for man to know what distance the human species are capable of covering between two Sundays, as it is for him to blindly believe that the sun is two million miles, one lap, four yards, three feet, and two inches from the earth. To sum up: the experiences of a 142 hours' trudge inculcates the necessity of a man refraining from over-indulgence in the pleasures of the world, the flesh, or the devil."

When we made our journey to the six day race in Sacramento, we were but part of a long tradition. We were sure there would also be some beer somewhere for Blower Brown's successors!

Gibson Ranch is a country park owned by Sacramento City but also lovingly looked after by the friends of the park who provide volunteers each weekend to help look after the place. It has a lake on which reside a great variety of geese and ducks and a small farmyard with horses, pigs, goats, sheep and chickens in a marvellous haphazard cacophony. It is a wonderful place for children at the weekends, for picnics, for horse riding and for the occasional athletic event. A main tarmacked circuit of just over a mile around the lake can be supplemented by additional circuits and there are also cross country tracks. Wooden cabins provide accommodation with 6/8 bunks per cabin with central washing, showering and toilet facilities.

In November this is supplemented by two large army style marquees. In one reside a team of lap counters and in the other volunteer cooks and helpers who are only too keen to mix up your own special concoction or provide whatever takes your fancy through the day or night. Marvellous evening dinners, including a Thanksgiving turkey roast with all the trimmings, plus seasoned marrows, chestnut stuffing - you name it they had it. There were vegetarian options and special local puddings all of which were designed either to provide you with a tremendous amount of fuel to keep you going all night or, alternatively, to bloat you so much that you fell asleep in the warm tent and never made it back outside.

With physiotherapists on call and feet specialist and others also in attendance, no wonder the event attracts people of all ages who come back year after year.

You would of course expect such high standards and deep understanding of runners' needs from the Kleins.

Norman Klein has for many years been the organiser and inspiration behind the Western States 100 miles cross mountain run. This premiere event attracts top ultra runners from all over the world who run, clamber, stagger and even wade across a fast flowing river and through terrain with such marvellous names as Squaw Valley and Cloud-topped Peak.

The whole event conjures up the frontier spirit, the individualism and the sheer drive and determination which is so much an aspect of the ultra distant runner.

Norman's wife, Helen Klein, is a remarkable lady. Charming and delightful she is also committed to proving that age is no barrier to athletic achievement. She is a living example of the doctrine espoused in a great book by Walter Bortz called *"We Live Too Short and Die Too Long"* that ageing is a self fulfilling prophecy. *"Most of us hold a severely negative stereotype of the ageing process"* with the medical profession, for example, being cure oriented, concerned with disease rather than health, with pills and potions rather than exercise and diet.

Walter Bortz admirably propounds the notion that for the equivalent of 23 hours and 59 minutes of our primate's 24 hour existence so far, we were active hunters and farmers. Our natural state is to be active, where "survival of the fittest" means precisely that. Only in our state of post industrial and service industry revolution laziness have we become like zoo animals being fed convenience foods, as we slump in our chairs in front of the TV or computer/video game.

Norman Cousins has put it admirably:

"Death is not the ultimate tragedy. Rather it is that which dies within us while we are still alive. "

A report in the Winter 1995 issue of "Population Trends" noted that while British men and women are living longer, those extra years may be far from productive. Healthy life expectancy for men aged 65 remained almost constant between 1976 and 1992 at about 7 years despite average life expectancy rising to 79. The figure for women increased by just one year, from 9 to 10 years, with an overall life expectancy of 83. Maybe this is not unrelated to the increase in the numbers of overweight men; up from 33% in 1980 to a staggering 43% in 1993.

With so many killer diseases from the past now conquered (such as TB), our modern killers and debilitators (such as heart disease and cancer) are closely related to our way of life. We can choose our diet; we can choose to give up or never take up smoking; we can choose to keep fit and healthy. Our healthy life expectancy is under our control.

We should all keep every particle of our mind and body active. We should be proud of the marvellous human form which has evolved and not abuse it. We should use it to its potential. Otherwise: *"if you don't use it, you loose it"*.

If you don't get out and use your walking, running, swimming or other muscles, they will slowly start to waste away. If you don't keep your mind active and alert you will slowly go to seed. Conversely, if you think positive, if you keep active both physically and mentally and if you set your sights on new targets ahead, then there is no reason why you should not remain mentally and physically fit and able to achieve what a previous generation thought was impossible, or inappropriate or just not conceivable for people in their 60's, 70's and 80's.

A report to the 1995 British Association conference by Professor Pat Robbitt of Manchester University noted that a group of superfit 70 year olds were just as mentally alert as those 20 years their junior. *"Jogging is better for the brain than doing crossword puzzles to keep people mentally alert in old age"* the study of more than 6,500 elderly people revealed. *"Jogging does probably all your brain good. "*

The American Medical Association reported earlier in 1995 the results of a 26 year study of 17,300 Harvard graduates from 1962 to 1988. This showed that the number of deaths was 25% lower amongst those taking vigorous exercise such as jogging, brisk walking, swimming or fast cycling.

For too long we have carried around mental baggage from previous generations which assume that once a person was in his or her 40's then you shouldn't be seen running in marathons, climbing mountains or playing rugby or cricket. "You're getting a bit past it, aren't you?" "Isn't it time you gave up this type of thing?" "You're not as young as you used to be you know," are phrases that still greet the person determined to maintain his or her fitness and "youthful" outlook on life. It might be all right to be seen on a golf course or a bowling green when you're in your 50's, but anything more energetic was thought of as being "non you" even dangerous to your health.

Sir John Astley had no doubts on the subject:

"All I can say is, I never knew of any man injuring his physique or constitution by a six days' tramp. I have always thought that I was badly treated by one good old gentleman at my club, who pathetically besought me one day to abandon a competition that I was just starting; saying: 'My dear Sir John, I feel sure you will be some day tried for manslaughter, when one of your competitors dies on the track.' I replied, 'Worthy sir, I will bet you "fifty," and leave it to our heirs and assigns to determine, that you die from want of exercise before any one of the competitors dies from taking too much. But, will you believe it? he would not book the bet, and quietly slipped into his grave (being short of exercise) some six months afterwards."

We now know that muscles thrive on activity. The heart, as a muscle, is no exception and continued activity and the maintenance of fitness lowers the long term risk of so many illnesses. Work carried out on us and other sports people at the Chelsea Hospital in London has shown that aorta flexibility (in the heart valves) can show no deterioration if physical activity is continued. The flexibility of someone in their 40's is the same as someone in their 20's.

Helen Klein is proof that it is never too late to start down the fitness and athletics route. It was only in her 60's that she decided to start running. Through continuous training and determination she now holds world records for long distance running at age bands from 60 to over 70.

"The animal world, except for us, lacks the insight and organised skills to alter destiny. Only we in our recognised universe have the capacity - the responsibility to see things as they might be and ask 'Why not?'." (Walter Bortz)

I suppose my father is another example of someone who does not so much "defy his age" as just not recognise it. He gets on with life regardless and ignores conventional wisdom about what could or should be done at any particular age. He was still fast bowling when he was 60 years of age and taking a good number of wickets for the local church cricket team. He was only finally persuaded to stop fast bowling by mother when he was hit in the face by a fast ball when fielding in the slips. He then took up under arm bowls. At the age of 90, he regularly beat players 10-15 years his junior and had enormous fun not revealing his age until the last minute to younger men of 85 who boasted about their age and what they were able to do.

I took him for his first flight in an aeroplane for his 80th birthday, with the result that, when he was 85, he took himself off to relations in Canada. It was the first time he had ever ventured overseas (except in the navy in the Second World War). He got a passport for the first time and I saw him off at Heathrow Airport clutching his little bag like some schoolboy going off for the first day to a new school. In Canada he flew around Ontario and Nova Scotia seeing relatives and friends and playing the grand old gentleman before returning full of stories to recount to all who would listen.

In October 1995 I took him to Italy for his 90th birthday. He had only crossed the English Channel once before in the Second World War. He was determined to talk to everyone - even though most people in the restaurant and cafes or historic sights of Verona had no English. He tucked into his pasta, made certain he got at least his half share of each bottle of wine and walked miles every day. But he would refuse to budge in the mornings until he had been brought his early cup of tea!

He has been a great inspiration I wonder what I will be doing when I am 90.

It was into the atmosphere which the Kleins have created

around Gibson Ranch that we descended in November 1994. I fear I did not do justice to the event or myself once I was affected by severe overnight cold and a biting wind at the end of the first day. For some reason I could not fully focus my mind on the event and be clear on what I was trying to achieve. I had failed to put into practice the lessons I had learnt and what I have set out in this book. I admit I failed to "walk my talk."

Sandra was also affected but, after a massage and a long rest in the warmth, came back to walk some 426 miles and proved to herself that she could handle a multi-day ultra event. From the third night, she was getting by on only about 1½ hours sleep per night and maintaining such a consistent walking pace that some of the runners took ages to catch her. Often, during the event, they would just jog along behind while she walked. No wonder some of them christened her *"the clockwork doll". "You just wind her up and away she goes at a steady pace until she starts to run out of fuel. She then stops for a quick refill in the tent, gets back on the circuit and immediately round and round she goes again at the same old steady pace."*

After the event, Norman and Helen Klein kindly took us back to their house and looked after us before our return flight from Sacramento. In the process, we became even greater converts to the point-to-point ultra distance event (such as the Western States) and with a renewed determination to have a go at the Lands End to John O'Groats records.

We had not been back a month when we had a phone call from John Foden, of the Road Runners Club. John is another tremendous father figure and advocate of ultra distance running. It was his inspiration that led to the creation in 1983 of the Spartathlon race.

Races are fond of tracing their pedigree, but few can upstage the Spartathlon. This commemorates the journey made by Pheidippides from Athens in 490BC to enlist the help of the Spartans against the invading Persians. This marvellous event of 246Km takes you along the coastal road before climbing overnight through the mountains, and the final run at dawn into Sparta and the traditional crowning with oak leaves of the victors.

John had been phoned by Countrywide Communications, who were acting for the company which had the distribution rights to the video version of Forrest Gump. In this American film, Forrest Gump (played by Tom Hanks) runs across the USA in search of some inner meaning to his life. In the process he gathers quite a following of those who found inspiration from just being out on the road with him. Some creative person in Countrywide had thought that it would be a good idea to try and find someone in the UK that might emulate Forrest Gump and run from one end of Britain to the other. They therefore contacted John Foden, who immediately thought of us. Little did he know he was providing the final spark that would inspire Sandra and I to commit ourselves to attempt a unique double.

We took our 9 year old daughter to see the film - it gave us a warm soft American glow. There was some marvellous technical wizardry in it which results in Tom Hanks shaking hands with American Presidents. It was also in keeping with our philosophy that any ordinary person can achieve great things. The run across the States and the gathering of others also made us think of all the friends we knew on route who might turn out and join in. We could make our run give at least a partial answer to Forrest's inner search by developing a "oneness" with everything and everyone we would come across.

It took us all of ten minutes when we got home to say "yes" and to phone John back. John was delighted (well he did not have to run it!) and put us directly in touch with Dan Holiday and Claire Donnelly at Countrywide.

The first meeting was fixed. No doubt they not only wanted to meet us but also size us up as to whether we stood any chance of lasting the course, whether we were vaguely presentable and whether we were capable of putting on a smile that could be acceptable to their clients and reproducible on TV and in the papers. The trouble was that this meeting was fixed for a lunchtime directly after I had been to the dentist to have a wisdom tooth removed. The result was that I arrived at Countrywide HQ, just off Hyde Park, with a very swollen mouth, unable to eat any of the lunch offered and with a swab cloth and cottonwool inside my mouth to soak up the blood oozing from where my wisdom tooth had been! Attempting to drink some water from a glass without either dribbling it down my numbed lips or dropping blood into the crystal clear water, I decided to minimise my Dracula like qualities and any intellectual input to the conversation by restricting myself to the occasional grunt.

Sandra waxed eloquent while downing her water and tuna sandwich but was somewhat restricted in the number of such sandwiches she could devour whilst still making conversation. Since neither of us drank any of the coffee, we ended up leaving a rather large lunch selection for the rest of the office. We had however apparently somehow passed the screen test.

We had also agreed a start date of dawn on Friday 5th May at Lands End. This date was as near as we could reasonably get to the 1st May, when Forrest Gump would be released on video in the UK. Our training schedule required us to have undertaken at least one 24 hour/200 kilometre race, as well as build up preparatory events, and also to allow sufficient time between that 24 hour event and the start of the Lands End to John O'Groats. The first 24 hour International Race-Walk would be at Lagny on 18th/19th March and three weeks between that race and an 830 miles was an absolute minimum.

Countrywide committed themselves and their clients to provide financial support of £4,000 against our bid of £6,000. They also undertook to provide two members for our support crews who would look after all publicity matters. Countrywide HQ would organise all media activities after consulting us. We agreed to organise everything else. We had less than 3 months in which to do it.

As I sat on the train going back to Bristol trying to hide my mouth, facial expressions and vampire-like qualities from the young innocent child sitting opposite, I wrote up the notes of a meeting I had held the previous evening at Bristol Zoo and looked through my lines before attending the first rehearsal that evening of the Chew Magna Society annual pantomime which this year was Jack and the Beanstalk. I was to be Giant Blunderbore. It all seemed slightly unreal. *"What have you done with him ... I'm so hungry I could eat a house, but a nice juicy young boy would be much better, and I'm sure I can sniff one around here somewhere."* I looked at the child opposite and covered my fangs which my handkerchief.

Back in Chew Magna I started to think of all the things we would have to do and how we couldn't hope to do them all without a lot of help. *"That's what you think; I've been terrorising these parts for the past thousand years or more, man and boy, and I'm not going to stop now. Giant Blunderbore always gets what he wants."* Yes, well, perhaps not.

In our Paris-Colmar races, we had always relied heavily on Peter Selby from Surrey Walking Club who had taken charge of the hiring of vans, booking of ferries, fixing of hotels, ordering of food, even the assembling of the crews themselves. But Peter was not available.

On my 1988 Lands End to John O'Groats run, a good friend and cross-country runner, Nigel Robinson, had helped in the organisation and had taken over as team leader once we started. Those had been the days when we were amateurish and had not properly planned and certainly had not appointed a Team Leader. I had tried to do most things myself and Nigel had seen from day one that I could not possibly control what was happening behind me in the vans and still focus on a record-breaking run. So although he had only intended to come with us for the first few days, he ended up taking charge and holding the whole thing together right the way to John O'Groats. Without his leadership and organisation we would not have made it, let alone broken the record.

We now needed a Team Leader that would take charge and relieve us of most of the worry and burden so we could focus on our training. We needed a Sir John Hunt in our assault on our Everest equivalent.

I would also need to liaise closely with that person because I alone had done the journey before and I also had the Paris-Colmar experiences. But I was now based in Bristol and there was no one within a hundred miles who had been either on a Paris-Colmar race or the Lands End to John O'Groats. I would therefore need to find someone that had the basic leadership and organisational skills plus the time and the energy; someone who was willing to learn as well as lead, someone that was pleasant and friendly and would get on well in a team but yet who was also tough enough to get things done. *"You wait 'til I get my hands on you, you evil smelling, pig swilling grockle sniffing little varmint you. And what's that you've got there? Why if it isn't my pride and joy, my hen that lays the golden eggs. Bertha, have had you anything to do with this?"* (Chase around stage to music and strobe lighting). No ... definitely

76

not that type of character.

I broached the potential of a record-breaking run as an aside to Doug Aitken as we showered at Welsh Back gym the next morning after our session on the weights and other machines of torture. Whether he felt slightly vulnerable as he stood naked under the shower, or just in a good mood, or just naively innocent, I don't know. But he managed to get himself sufficiently caught in the web I was weaving that by the time he had dried himself I knew I had the manager we needed.

Doug Aitken had been in charge of National Westminster Bank's Registrars Department in Bristol. When NatWest had sold out a few weeks earlier, he had taken his package and run. At the gym, he was the one person either sufficiently awake in the mornings or a sufficient team player to gather a small group of us around him for the occasional jog around the Floating Harbour in the centre of the city. It was Doug who smiled and welcomed new faces to our 7 am sessions and who seemed to be on good terms with everyone at such an ungodly hour. Yet he was obviously a firm and thinking manager with financial control skills that would be important. The only question in my mind was whether his occasional abrasive firmness might rub some people up the wrong way. But firmness would be needed.

I introduced him gently to the enormity of the task and he went away to write down some thoughts.

When we met in a couple of days time, I was hardly prepared for the rigour of his approach. As a business planner myself, I am used to constructing vision statements, the supporting strategies and action plans and securing the involvement and commitment necessary if implementation throughout an organisation is to be achieved. I was ready to indoctrinate Doug with the rigorous planning approach we would need. But Doug took the wind out of my sails:

"I have drafted this mission statement. Have a think about it. Talk to Sandra over the weekend and let's agree something on Monday."

Fantastic. We did not change his draft. It read:

"To cover the distance, on foot, from Lands End to John O'Groats faster than has been previously achieved and to benefit a chosen charity." Doug also started to identify who were our key

stakeholders and what they were likely to want from their involvement.

We set down, after some discussion, the following objectives:

Runners *(Richard and Sandra)*	*To set new World Records*
Financial	*To make the most effective use of our sponsor's financial support*
	To maximise the financial benefit for the chosen charity
	To manager our finances effectively
Publicity	*To maximise the event's charity fundraising potential*
	To give our sponsors maximum exposure
Support Crew	*To undertake a uniquely satisfying adventure as part of a team effort*
	To proactively provide at all times the assistance the runners will require.
	To ensure that no time is lost due to mismanagement of the programme.

We recognised that the sponsors, the charity, and other stakeholders may have additional objectives. We would need to recognise these, but we agreed they must not distract from the overall mission.

An Organisation Chart helped us determine the roles and responsibilities of the various players. And we highlighted how we should try and break down the various major tasks, and which ones should be under Doug and which entirely independent.

We all agreed, for example, that the team would have enough

TEAM LEADER

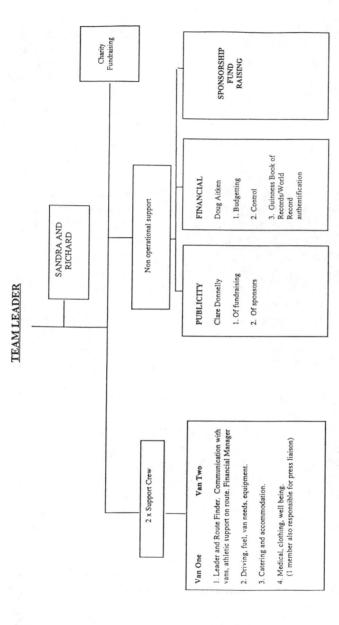

SANDRA AND RICHARD

Charity Fundraising

Non operational support

2 x Support Crew

PUBLICITY

Clare Donnelly

1. Of fundraising

2. Of sponsors

FINANCIAL

Doug Aitken

1. Budgetting

2. Control

3. Guinness Book of Records/World Record authentification

SPONSORSHIP FUND RAISING

Van One   Van Two

1. Leader and Route Finder. Communication with vans, athletic support on route. Financial Manager

2. Driving, fuel, van needs, equipment.

3. Catering and accommodation.

4. Medical, clothing, well being. (1 member also responsible for press liaison)

1. Van One leader to be in overall charge, but both vans must be independent ivo pre event organisation and differing needs of runners; and both teams must be self-sufficient

2. Laision with other clubs prior to the event is responsibility of Richard and Sandra; team to input ideas

3. We need to ensure those people to be involved have necessary skills

to do without trying to organise fundraising for a major charity. We therefore felt that whatever charity was chosen, they would have to be entirely self-contained and have to look after their own campaign. We would lend such support as we could, but not if it distracted us in any way from our prime objective.

We would also have to be firm with our major sponsor. For example, we could not deviate from the final route we might chose for photo opportunities. Interviews on the run would also have to respect our prime record-breaking objective. We would have our work cut out focusing on that.

In the event, both our sponsor and our chosen charity were marvellous in the way they got on efficiently with their own tasks, supported what we were doing (and indeed provided great encouragement) but in no way distracted us from our task.

I was also clear that, although it would impose great responsibilities on Doug, he had to assume total management control. Sandra and I could offer advice and experience and suggestions, but there had to be one boss. If we got sucked into the organisational side, it would be fatal. We would end up being distracted from training, with split responsibilities and with our team not knowing to whom they should look for decisions. Some issues would then fall between the cracks and everyone would end up blaming everyone else.

The organisational structure shown opposite placed Doug firmly in charge.

Having set the mission and the key objectives, we now set about identifying the other key players and establishing action plans on who was going to do what and by when.

We quickly identified a financial controller in Ann Pryer. Ann, or Annie as her answerphone announces, was a regular attendee at our Welsh Back gym sessions. She was a flat mate of Debbie, who was soon to "volunteer" as one of our enthusiastic crew members. Most important, she was an accountant at Coopers & Lybrand in Bristol. She set about establishing a separate bank account with her, Doug and I as signatories and started to outline three budgets: a best case, worst case and most likely outcome.

Over the next few weeks, we started to fill in the figures largely on the basis of information which Doug was gathering. They made worrying reading.

The best we could hope for was to maintain costs to just over £6,000; but that assumed we would get two vans free, one at half price and hence only have to pay the full cost of one for two weeks. (We would need that amount of time to get down to the start, do the run, turn around rest and then drive all the way back from the North of Scotland). At around £900 for each van (more if we lost the damage deposit) the vans would be the major item of expenditure. It seemed very optimistic to assume that most of this cost would be met.

In the worst case, costs were over £10,000 (and we could have constructed a worse, worst case under which for example all four vans sustained some minor knocks - from overhanging tress on camp sites or scratches in narrow lanes, as had happened to one of our vans on my previous Lands End to John O'Groats run - and hence we would have to forfeit all or part of the damage deposits). The thought that we might need longer than two weeks never entered the equation; though with the women's record at over 13½ days perhaps it should have done. But then the costs would have been even higher.

Our base plan suggested costs of at least £7,200. This however assumed we would get two vans free on the basis of leverage from a national charity. Without that it would be nearer £9,000. I mentally prepared myself for £9,000 and got ready to break into the piggy bank.

While the £4,000 sponsorship via Countrywide was vital in helping meet the costs of the run (indeed without such support it could not have taken place since Sandra and I would have had to have found between £7,000 and £9,000 out of post tax income) even so, we were faced with a likely additional bill of between £3,000 and £5,000. Somehow we had to reduce this.

The most likely way was either to find a national charity which had access to or could lean on a van provider, or to go to another corporate sponsor who would provide some support on condition that we would chose his organisation's favourite charity. Small items of support to defray some of the costs (such as free food and drink, reduced price meals at roadside chains on the route, free overnight camp sites and use of showers, reduced price petrol, anything .... please! ...) would help. It would however take a tremendous amount of time and effort to garner in such support.

Our preferred way was therefore to try and get a single major additional financial input.

It is extremely difficult to get sponsorship. When Sandra and I did the Paris-Colmar races in France, we wrote letters to many organisations. However, because the race was in France, was little known in the UK, and there would be very limited TV and press coverage, there was virtually no interest. One year we got £1,000 from British Coal.

We seemed to be better known in France than in the UK. Articles in magazines such as L'Equipe, the French sports magazine, focused on our unique husband and wife athletic partnership. One of their articles played the stereotyped picture of the Brit overseas for all it was worth but with good humour:

"Two English people on the Continent" was the headline. "To walk alone is good, to walk as a pair is better ... with the peculiarity that apart from having to drive on the right, there is always a teapot on the hob of course," "The only time they were seen together was at the start. Photo time, click, click and Sandra leaves her husband without further formalities. Apart from 'Bye, Darling, see you at the finish,' such style."

Other French press coverage has been either in a similar vein or of the soap opera variety.

Under the heading *"Marche Nuptiale"* (Wedding March) a provincial French newspaper described our joint win at an international race near Rheims.

"The weather, more typically English than French, did not prevent Richard Brown from winging his way to victory. A wife must always walk by her husband's side. If the wife was sometimes overtaken by her husband on the circuit, the couple were to be found once more in each others arms on the steps of the podium after little Sandra had won the women's race."

So much for women's lib in France!

Not that perhaps our British team manager was much better than the French press in being a caricature of the Englishman abroad. He insisted on pronouncing the French village around which the race was centred as Bajincourt to rhyme with Agincourt. This seemed entirely appropriate when the National Anthem floated over the fields of France following my victory to be followed a few moments later by a repeat performance when Sandra crossed the line to win the women's event. But I'm not certain his pronunciation endeared him to the French!

Through my French connections while working at Meyer International, I managed to get over £1,000 from the Poliet Group. They own the largest chain of builders' merchants in France, "Point P", just as Meyer own the largest chain in the UK, "Jewson". So our British support crews travelled across France advertising a French builders' merchants chain on their tee shirts and with the name "Point P" emblazoned across our vans.

When I joined the National Grid Company, our opposite numbers on the international side of Electricite de France (EDF) seemed to know all about this British husband and wife team. They offered over £1,000 for us to walk in their colours. I had earlier been refused support by the relevant committee at the National Grid. But when the Chairman, David Jefferies, heard that I was about to walk across France with an EDF flag flying, he cut through the bureaucracy and generously matched the French offer. So an athletic partnership between EDF and NGC was consummated on the road to Colmar.

Fyonna Campbell, whom we were delighted to meet before her great African walk and to try and give her such advice as we could, has described both at the start and again later on in her book "Walking Across Africa" the difficulties she has had in raising funds. I think she is right when she says that sponsors don't want to run the risk of being associated with any failure and hence shy away from supporting individual exploits. They have a risk aversion which often prevents them supporting the adventurous.

Risk aversion is a dreadful disease. It can cripple the most entrepreneurial company. When accountants and others of a like mind get hold of a group by the throat, it can be terminal. There is also a danger of it spreading. Fortunately, the accountants were in the back room when Brunel built the GWR and launched the largest steamship in the world. They probably didn't exist when John Cabot persuaded Bristol merchants to back his voyage 500 years ago across the Atlantic and discover not just a collection of islands in the Caribbean as Christopher Columbus had done, but the coast of North America.

US companies in Silicon Valley spring up and expand all the time on the basis of risk capital. Some entrepreneurs evidently find it easier to secure such support if they have undergone the experience of business failure; the logic is that they will have learnt from that failure.

In any case, what is "failure"? Did Captain Scott "fail" in his attempt on the South Pole?"

"Had we lived, I should have had a tale to tell of the hardihood, endurance and courage of my companions which would have stirred the hearts of every Englishman. These rough notes and our dead bodies must tell the tale."

These were about the last words Captain Scott wrote in his diary.

Cannot creative marketing people turn anything into positive coverage for their company? Is not a feat of endurance in which people get up out of their armchairs and push their body and mind to the limits something which can excite press coverage and benefit the sponsoring company? The interest which National TV, radio, press and their regional equivalents showed in the Gump Run suggests that tremendous value can be created. I hope and believe that our sponsor was delighted with the coverage Forrest Gump secured.

I suggest that all companies need to consider how such sponsorship can play a role in their overall marketing and image creating strategy. The likely exposure and returns from such sponsorship need to be considered alongside the cost of just a single advert in a national daily, or a hospitality suite at Wimbledon, or a box at the opera. It has its part to play in a total marketing mix. If companies are really concerned about individuals, then I hope they will increasingly back individuals who show their individuality. Let them put down what after all is a relatively small amount of risk capital and then play it for all it is worth.

We were not successful in getting additional major sponsorship. Partly this was because our main sponsor CIC did not want their message and the focus on their product - The Forrest Gump video - to be diluted. Hence placards or names on the vans or on support crews' tee shirts were not possible. Without that, we had no real sales pitch or offering to make to a sponsor.

One charity was interested in putting some money up front in return for coverage on the vans, in the press and as part of a major fundraising campaign. They would have expected to have recouped their input many times over. This might well have been acceptable to CIC. But by then we were well down the road with another national charity SPARKS.

SPARKS stands for Sports Aiding Medical Research for Kids. It was founded by top sports personalities to help children to be born healthy and stay healthy. It raises funds through a wide range of fun sporting events in order to finance medical research projects at hospitals and universities throughout Britain.

SPARKS has its headquarters a few hundred yards away from our home in Westminster. Sandra and I had first come across them when we were helping to organise the Westminster 200 Km Paris-Colmar qualifying international race-walk in Battersea Park in 1993. In the time available, they had not been able to mount much of a display, but some leaflets and sponsorship forms had been sent with information on the race to all competitors and more leaflets were handed out during the event.

Sandra and I now had a meeting with their director, Hugh Peers, a charming retired naval captain, and some of his extremely enthusiastic and pleasant team. The fact that one of them, Angela Dudley, had parents just round the corner from Doug Aitken and quite often visited them, was a bonus. We said we would be delighted if they could be our chosen charity and that we would be pleased to carry their banners, wear their tee shirts and give them such coverage as we could. Equally, we made it clear that they would have to look after their own fundraising. They entirely understood and threw themselves with great vigour at planning what they might do to raise their exposure from one end of Britain to the other. It seemed an excellent opportunity for them and they felt that spreading their name was as important as actually raising cash. The latter would not be easy given that Sandra and I would only be passing through a few towns and otherwise would mainly have sheep and cows as onlookers.

Hugh and his colleagues hoped they might be able to provide some help with vans and even hotels for the odd overnight stay and shower for the crew. In the event, nothing much materialised on that front. They did however help raise the profile of the event considerably and I hope achieved their main objective of further raising awareness of their marvellous organisation which does so much to help children that have been less fortunate than ourselves or our daughter, Victoria.

Olympic Gold Medallists, Steve Cram and Sally Gunnell both pledged their support to us. Sally recorded a message on an 0891 number (which itself generates funds for the charity) and in return for answering a couple of simple questions, the caller could win a state of the art combined TV and video recorder. Steve Cram recorded an interview which was incorporated into the pre-race pack sent to national and regional TV stations - in which he also said he thought we were mad! Angela Dudley and a couple of her SPARKS colleagues were also to turn out for part of the route and even Hugh himself made the effort, not only to join us in Welsh Border country but also to walk briskly by my side for a couple of miles on the way to Hereford.

Some additional financial support did arise. West Country Motor Homes, near Axbridge south of Bristol, most generously discounted the price of one of the two vans we hired from them by over 50%. Their brand new vehicles proved excellent and trouble free.

Would the same could be said for Knightcott of Weston-Super-Mare. One of their vans should probably never have been hired out in the first place. Battery and alternator failures meant that until it could be repaired properly on day three, it had to be push started every morning and every time it stopped. Woe betide anyone who stalled it on a hill! The whole electrical circuits could not be relied on. This was to cause real and unnecessary aggro at the start of the event. Knightcott appeared reluctant to make the effort and come to repair the vehicles, while the breakdown cover turned out to be largely irrelevant given the age of the vehicles. Later we also found the toilets did not work properly and one of the roofs leaked.

Doug wrote many letters to hotels and camp sites we would pass on route and the Talbot Hotel in the centre of Leominster (an old coaching inn with great charm and black beams) which we literally passed right in front of, kindly offered us a free room for the night. Various camp sites also offered us free or cheap parking (though not in Scotland where the canny locals even charged us for refilling our water tanks).

We went back to our budgets and trimmed them further

wherever we could. Even so, with us now having to meet virtually the full cost of four vans for two weeks, we were facing total outgoings of over £8,000. Doug therefore went back to Countrywide who spoke to CIC. They I am sure appreciated our financial position (we exposed all figure work to them) and were also benefiting from prior publicity. So a week before we started, they offered a further £1,000. This was not only a great relief, but also added to the positive atmosphere that was increasingly spreading through the team.

We were delighted to be able to christen the run "The Forrest Gump Run" after our sponsors and to put in a lot of work with them to ensure they got exceptional value for their money. (We tried in other words to practice what we preached about "delighting" customers).

Hence we went to Land's End on a cold, wet, windy weekend to "put in the can" the start and various sequences around Land's End. (The fact that our actual start was during a heatwave made a bit of a mockery of this sequence and I never knew what use the TV stations made of it). Sandra also got a recorded interview with the Chancellor of the Exchequer, Kenneth Clarke, who kindly donated £10 to SPARKS. Various shots were taken inside the Treasury and the distributors of the Gump Run video did their promotional sequence against a suitably ornate and august Treasury interior. They seemed delighted ... as well they should!

On the run we also responded to all requests for interviews. Panting into a mobile phone may not have produced smooth flowing conversation but at least it gave atmosphere.

So we tried wherever we could to adopt an "inclusive" approach and try and satisfy the needs of our stakeholders so that a win-win feeling was created and everyone felt they had gained.

Let me summarise:

Great achievements don't just happen. They require years of planning, years of dedication and build up. Sometimes the vision is almost lost but if the will to reach it is there, it will re-emerge from the mist and you will again be drawn to it.

Age need be no barrier. It is not just a question of "you are as old as you feel" but also an issue of "how old are you if you didn't know how old you are?"

Any major project needs not only its champions but also its team leader. That person has to be the focal point for all decisions. The leader has to lead a team approach to a clearly defined objective. That involves identifying and satisfying the stakeholders, co-ordinating the plan of campaign and raising and controlling the funding and other resources necessary. Certain tasks will be delegated, but the leader must be the final arbiter.

Financial planning and fund raising targets are particularly important.

I suggest all targets should be:

- focused and few in number
- clear and comprehensible by all involved
- measurable
- relevant and output not input driven
- stretching but achievable
- be bought into by the key players
- take account of past experience (continuity) and comparative data (benchmarking)
- be cost effective

Targets should also be monitored regularly and adapted where necessary in the light of changing experiences.

The focus however must always be on the prime objective. Secondary objectives must remain secondary. Intermediate targets and milestones are not ends in themselves. The margin between success and relative failure is too small to allow compromises.

8

Creating a Winning Team

Just as armies walk on their stomachs and are only as good as their logistic support, so multi-day expeditions depend on their teams to get them to their destinations. You can have all the motivation in the world, but that motivation is in the mind, and the mind has to be accompanied by a body which needs basic sustenance. Only a well organised and committed team can supply that.

The mind also needs support and encouragement. We are social animals and need to interact with others. When things get difficult, we gain renewed momentum from those around us, from sharing, talking about and thinking through a problem and agreeing a way forward. Without this interaction, we retreat as individuals into a selfish shell.

It requires a special type of person with a dedication no less than our own to work well with others with single-mindedness of purpose in difficult cramped conditions for up to two weeks. It is thanks to their commitment that the records were broken. The new records set were their records as much as ours.

We had agreed earlier with Doug that, while all the financial planning was underway, Sandra and I would work on recruiting the crews that were to be our life support system. We knew who the likely contenders were. With Doug, we had listed the roles which had to be performed by crew members and hence the essential skills and experience they needed.

We required four people per van. Between them they would have to drive navigate, walk/run/cycle alongside us handing over food and drink, prepare that food and drink, offer changes of clothes (especially if it rained), get regular sightings for the Guinness Book of Records to meet their accreditation procedures, have some physiotherapy and ideally relevant medical experience as well as remaining motivated, cheerful, giving positive feedback to us and working well as a team. Simple really!

Within each crew there would need to be a van leader and there would also need to be a team leader for Sandra's crews (Doug was the natural leader of mine).

We turned first to those that had relevant experience. Nigel Robinson, who had led the crew in my 1988 run, was unfortunately committed to support his ultra-distance wife, Eleanor in a 48 hour run in Western France. He was nevertheless to turn out on his return, driving straight from having left Eleanor and their son, Myles (what other name for the son of two ultra-distance runners?) at their home near the Roman wall to join me for a couple of hours as I crossed the Scottish border. He was then to return the next day to support Sandra. Such is the camaraderie in the ultra-distance fraternity.

Amos Seddon, had won a medal for race-walking at the Commonwealth Games and had supported me on the Paris-Colmar, I knew he would be a decisive and firm van leader. I hoped that Don Thompson and his colleague Derek Appleton would accept his sometimes blunt style while reciprocating his tremendous commitment. Don had won a Gold medal in the 50 km walk at the Rome Olympics in 1960. He had been christened "Mighty Mouse" by the Italians and has remained true to this description as he scuttled about on long distance walks and runs or escaping from his house before dawn on most days to scamper around the Kentish lanes in training.

My earliest memory of an athlete training was seeing Don prepare for the Rome Olympics. We had just acquired a TV set and I remember watching the strange sight of someone in their bathroom, surrounded by kettles of steaming hot water and electric heaters, training in the type of humid, hot conditions that would have been encountered in the Rome Olympics. Little did I know that I was, in the years to come, to be competing with this highly committed athlete in long distance race-walk internationals in the UK and overseas and to have his enthusiastic support and pacing on our World-beating Gump Run.

If Doug was to be a van leader, he needed at least one experienced supporter. Unfortunately Thierry Masson of Surrey Walking Club, who had been on many ultra-distance walks as participant and supporter, had to withdraw a week before the event.

Cyril Watmore was therefore asked to move across from one of Sandra's vans to join Doug. He was to prove literally a pillar of strength when I had to lean on his shoulder to help me down the steep incline towards Inverness, as my knee swelled like a pumpkin.

Debbie Morris (the flatmate of our financial controller, Annie) was terrifically keen to join in the adventure. She was part of our early morning Welsh back team. So was Lucy Hares, who kept asking whether there was room in the squad. She was to join Sandra's team at Warrington since she could not spare the whole two weeks, "And I've never been to Scotland and am really looking forward to it".

Boyd Millen was the first fell runner to do a Bob Graham double round of the Lake District, had been in Paris-Colmar support crews and is as wiry and as tough as they come. He coached his wife when she was an international race walker and also has some medical knowledge.

Glynis Kirkpatrick is a member of the Long Distance Walkers Association and has also been in Paris-Colmar support crews. Through sheer mental determination she has fought off cancer and continued her long distance walking and support at events. She provides a model of determination and conviction in a very different way.

Sue Ramsay is also a long distance walker and was to be the great find of the team. Quite unassuming, terribly conscientious and concerned and sympathetic to Sandra's needs, she was increasingly to take over van leadership responsibilities, go all the way to John O'Groats when others had to leave and then write back volunteering for more expeditions and making suggestions for improving the approach "in case you thought of doing it again".

Jill and Dave Green and Roger Moss also come out of the Long Distance Walkers Association stable. Jill was the first grandmother to complete the Paris-Colmar walk and has notched up consistent long distance performances in many French races. Her husband Dave often supports her. Roger Moss and John Robinson had survived my previous end-to-end run and now volunteered for more.

Roy and his brother Cyril Watmore were Paris-Colmar veterans, and our crews were completed by Ian and Lizzie from

Countrywide Communications.

We had thus assembled a team of people who could drive, cycle, run, walk, cook, navigate and take sightings for the Guinness Book of Records. But we had no specialist medical back-up. Three or four of the team were good at massage but we needed a specialist physiotherapist who could also analyze more serious muscular problems. Ideally, he would bring a portable ultra-sound for deep muscle tensions and would also have some capability to look after blisters and other problems that would affect the feet. We had found on Paris-Colmar walks that the feet were the most vulnerable part. If they really disintegrated, then we would grind ever slower and eventually have to stop. It would have been nice to have paid a podiatrist to join us as we had on the Paris-Colmar event. But we could not afford one.

Initially our medical support was to be Jim Booth from the Royce Clinic in Bath who had treated me for some lower back stiffness. However, he had to pull out virtually at the last minute. Fortunately, we were put in touch with James Tomkies. This energetic and highly committed physio is a tri-athlete and keen to learn more about what drives people to do apparently insane acts of endurance. He was to find out more in the days to come as we walked together in the fading light around the Cheshire countryside and again in darkness down to the Cromarty Firth.

James and I had a briefing session in a local pub. Over my orange and lemonade and his diet Coke, I tried to lead him in gently to what would be in store. We needed him. But there was no point in securing him under totally false pretences. His commitment otherwise would soon wane and if he deserted us en route we would really be left in it.

"Well it all sounds very exciting but also very daunting. I must put together a whole pack of different medical dressings and see about that ultra-sound. How much money can I spend on medical equipment?" He was hooked.

On the event he was to prove utterly dependable, so conscientious that I was afraid he would wear himself out as he cycled, ran and walked and seemed to move from one shift to the other. He was so competent with his tapes and strappings and second skin that I was by the end walking on what he had created underneath and around my swollen blistered feet.

The team on whom records depend.

Above, with my record breaking crew in 1988, left to right: Simon, Mojo, Lorraine, Nigel and John.

Below, relaxing after our successful 1995 adventure with, left to right: James, Derek, Cyril, Amos and Doug.

Above, Sandra swings through France on the Paris–Colmar race with Tony and Kathy.

Below, After our unique joint win in the UK national 100 mile racewalking championship at Leicester in 1992.

Above left, a rather tired and wet Daddy gets support from the ever enthusiastic Victoria in the 1993 national 50Km racewalk.

Above right, in happier mood winning the 1995 national 100 mile racewalking championships.

Below, Sandra on her way to another victory in the women's section of the national 100 mile championship.

Above, from Land's End to *below* the Forth Bridge, only a few hours separated us, and in Devon and Cornwall *inset* only a few yards.

Above, alright for some! The SPARKS charity crew with Boyd (second left) relax while *below* James and I face the headwind and onset of snow north of Aviemore.

Above, "I'm just going for a walk, I may be gone some time." With a displaced patella, not able to run and caught in the cold, it was a crisis in the snow.

Below, the feet begin to show the effects.

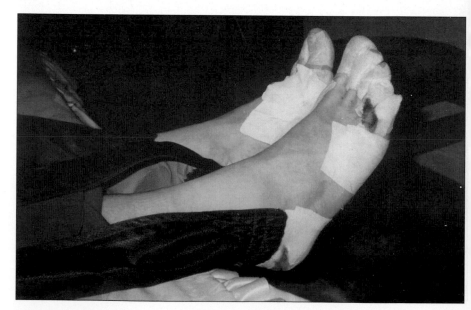

Above, Don Ritchie, whose record I was beating, turns out to support me; such is the camaraderie among ultra-distance athletes.

Below, Sandra celebrates her record with flowers and champagne.

Above, Norris McWhirter, with his brother the joint founding editors of the Guinness Book of Records, hands over a copy of the 1996 edition.

Below, The Institute of Human Development's pack for self-assessment motivation programme "Releasing Your Potential".

Settling the crews had proved more harrowing than we had intended. To have a couple of last minute drop-outs was particularly unfortunate.

We nevertheless had a balance of experienced ultra-distant supporters, enthusiastic newcomers who were eager to learn and contribute. We also had a balance of the sexes. It may be a sexist thing to suggest, and I am certainly open to persuasion on this point, but I had felt that a young woman in the crew somehow helps the men to give that little bit extra, to be less jostling for position and able to work better as a team. This may just reflect my own personal preference. It may, however, also be that an all-female crew may not work quite so well as a team that has a man in it. What is certain is that there will be tensions in any team. It will take time for a crew to settle into a pattern of working together with each member having the boundaries of his or her role fully understood and with everyone fully contributing. Anything which minimises the length of time it takes to achieve team coherence and the team spirit should be welcomed.

Normally the credits come at the beginning or end of a film. I have however listed the crews here because they are not some add-on to an individual performance. The team effort is central to a team achievement. Our mixture of experienced Paris-Colmar supporters supplemented by enthusiasts eager to learn and contribute was to prove a world-beating combination. It is like an acrobatic formation - a pyramid up which you clamber. All eyes may go to the small figure standing at the top, but that person is only there because of the strong shoulders and sure footing of those below. It is the mutual interplay of determination and motivation and the confidence that results that enables the person to climb to the top of the pyramid. Hilary and Tensing stick the flag on Everest thanks to the efforts and inspiration of their colleagues. An individual's Everest is achieved by the same route.

Every individual has his or her strengths and weaknesses. A team becomes more than the sum of its individuals when the complementary skills interact, bring out the best in everyone and create a virtuous circle of positive, enthusiastic, professionalism.

Meredith Belbin is his book "Management Teams - why they succeed or fail" notes how a team can combine all the qualities necessary for success which one individual alone cannot possess.

He identified eight key team roles (such as Chairperson, the creative/innovative "plant," the "completer/finisher") which he felt were essential to effectiveness. Each was associated with a particular type of personality. The mix of personalities therefore had a major bearing on the outcome of a team's effort to reach its objective.

He concluded that, given adequate knowledge of the personal characteristics and abilities of team members as derived from psychometric tests, the likely results could be forecast. Some teams would gel with the individuals reacting well and being mutually supportive so that positive results were achieved. In others the inner tensions and lack of some key skills meant there was a fatal flaw, one or two links in the chain were missing. Unsuccessful teams, he felt, could be improved by analysing their team design shortcomings and making appropriate changes.

He tested his theories on the Oxford University Strategic Leadership Programme which I attended in 1988 with a game "Teamopoly." Judging by the fact that our unbalanced team of innovative "plants" began to fly apart as the creative forces were given full rein, I think his point was proved. We only stayed in the game through using our innovation to rob the bank, having distracted the innocent banker!

There is of course a danger that such theories can be taken to extremes with pseudo scientific categorisation of individuals. In practice, we are more complicated than any psychometric classification (be it the 16PF or any other type). Equally a team has a dynamic momentum which will reflect the external changes and pressures upon it.

However the basic point has a validity which is all too often neglected. As individuals we do have particular traits and particular strengths. A team which has different individuals with strengths appropriate for the job in hand will work better and more cohesively than one where, for example, everyone wants to lead, or where there are lots of ideas but no one can take decisions or where no one can be bothered to attend to the details and hence the grand plan falls apart for lack of effective implementation.

There is a great danger that leaders select their teams from people with similar personalities, people with whom a leader can easily associate with. As someone with lots of ideas and the enthusiasm to get on and try and implement a hundred and one of them, all at the same time, I need a down to earth accountant or someone of a similar ilk to force me to think through the priorities, assess the resource implications and then discard 90% of the ideas or store them for another occasion.

The other major lesson I learnt from Belbin's work was the importance of building on strengths, not trying to change people by focusing on deficiencies. A well built team would provide the balance and rounded skills needed. An individual need not, and indeed probably could not, encapsulate all the skills needed.

The Civil Service training seemed so often to be aimed at overcoming weaknesses, at plugging gaps in your own capabilities, at making you an all-things-to-all-men type of standard generalist clone. The concept seemed to be of developing a "safe pair of hands," someone who would loyally carry out his duty for about 3 years in one post and then equally do well in a completely different area of a Government Department. There was little attempt to build on people's strengths and, say, focus a person's career on marketing or promotional work, or on legislation, or on speech writing and information dissemination, or on financial control or human resource issues. The generalist remained the ideal.

It is important that everyone has a good grounding in basic transferable skills such as numeracy, IT, problem solving, inter personal relations and oral and written expression. The Civil Service approach thus has its strengths, especially in an age when flexibility is needed so changing job requirements can be satisfied. Over specialisation could be a road to a dead end job. Life long learning and self development and training plans are still for many companies and individuals unfortunately concepts rather than realities.

But should a job in finance just be part of general training? A post in a Civil Service Personnel Department often meant you were not thought much of and nobody particularly wanted you. The concept of "human resources" being the lifeblood of a Government Department, of staff as assets needing to be appropriately supported, trained, harnessed and enthused by professionally trained personnel seemed not to have caught on!

Some better balance may be needed between general

transferable skills and a focus on a specialism. Otherwise too many public servants will find they have little relevant expertise for life beyond the security guard.

It is not always possible of course to build the ideal team. You often have to work with the raw material you have or that is around. Tensions will arise. Sometimes you inherit a team and there are limits as to how far you can change it. It may take months before you can achieve the balance of skills and personalities you would prefer. In other cases a team has to be thrown together from the resources available. Provided the pool of talent available to you is broad enough, then this can however be a tremendous opportunity.

As the security of a life long job in one organisation disappears and flexibility and movement increasingly becomes the norm, so the potential for building the preferred team increases. Accepting what you have inherited should not be used as an excuse for failing to build the team on which success depends.

A strong team, a strong organisation will (in the words of the book by Richard Pascale) *"manage on the edge"* between creative tension and learning. It will maintain a restless drive to question and improve, without descending into anarchic conflict. *"Constructive contention"* should continually *"power the engine of enquiry"*.

One of the greatest tests of the true leader is whether he or she can create a vibrant, questioning and innovative team that is always pushing out its boundaries and yet remains together in its commitment and drive to reach the clear agreed objective. While we did not want too much questioning and innovation in our crews (!), it was significant that Doug's team which had the least experienced members, seemed to knit best together with everyone slotting into a specific role and carrying that out with enthusiasm and bonhomie. It says much for Doug, his pre race briefing and his management style of leading as much from behind and by example as from out in front, that the blend of skills he put together worked so well.

The book "The Soul of a Machine" describes how a project team was pulled together to work outside the official corporation mould on what was to become the micro computer on which Data General's fortunes in the 1980s were to be built. The motor industry and other sectors also have similar stories to tell of creative teams being pulled together from across different functions to produce world beating products or ideas in a time span not thought possible. A crisis can indeed produce a response. What a shame it often seems to need the crisis to shake senior management out of its accepted ways of doing things. Success has the seeds of its own disaster if it leads (like an IBM or a GM or so many of the "success" stories in "In Search of Excellence") to rigidity, playing safe, and sticking so close to the knitting that the pattern is never questioned, and changing customer preferences and future needs never adequately reassessed.

I would not want to pretend that our teams for the Gump Run were ideal in every respect. You do not always know how some people will interact. Certainly not how they will blend in close confinement in a campervan for day after day. Placid, unconcerned passengers might mix; but they would not have the go-go qualities needed to motivate Sandra and myself, be alive to every route marking, every half hour feed and enticing nutritional offer; they would not be on the edge of their seats, on that delicate line between creative enthusiasm and destructive individualism. Perhaps Sandra's crews needed stronger leadership. Their commitment and concern was never in doubt, but was it fully focused and energised?

I prefer the enthusiasts any time, plus the leader who can, where necessary, direct that energy in a positive direction. It may be one of my weaknesses, and the reverse side of my enthusiastic streak, that I want to see activity, whereas there are times when reflection and an easy acceptance of things as they are may be more appropriate.

On the Forrest Gump run I was occasionally to show frustration and annoyance to my crews. I would immediately regret it; but the words had slipped out, the frown had been made and the actions could not be undone. Under tension we can all let a less temperate and pleasant side of our character slip out. Further training in relaxation and a more holistic approach to life's long race is needed. I still have a lot of practising to do. But then I have the second half of my life in which to improve!

So I suggest you should:

Choose a team which has a mixture of complementary skills and personalities.

Ensure you have a core of relevant expertise.

Ideally chose people that have worked together before and have a known rapport. The team will bed down faster that way, though you have to avoid the risk of cliquishness; everyone has to feel they are as valuable as everyone else and have a distinct role to play.

Allocate tasks and ensure everyone knows about and is happy with the role assigned and the roles of others.

Get the team together as soon as practicable and keep them informed of what is happening. That way they will feel involved right from the start.

Encourage them to inject their own thoughts and experience. This is not only valuable in that it will improve the plan of campaign, but will also increase their commitment.

Getting team members to think themselves into their new roles will reduce the element of surprise and hence the slope of the learning curve when the show finally does get on the road.

9

Going for the Record

When Don Ritchie "borrowed" my end-to-end record and lowered it by under three hours I was annoyed. We had reduced it by a substantial margin and had not bothered too much about the odd few minutes here and there.

After I had written to Don, I thought of all the quarter of an hours we had wasted going off course to stay with friends, or finding a bed in a hotel or bed and breakfast. I vowed there and then that we would only sleep in our vans and that they would stop either in laybys or as close as possible to the route if that was not practical and we were on busy noisy roads, for example.

I also thought of the time that we had spent at the beginning and end of each day massaging muscles and repairing feet. Was there any way we could save some of that time? In 1988 we had used a portable ultra-sound machine when the calf muscles had started to cause problems. This had no doubt been necessary at the time, but it had meant finding hotels or other places with power-points where we could plug in the machine. Could we get away without ultra-sound? Perhaps we should have one for an emergency, but otherwise rely on physiotherapy. It would be even better if the muscles could hold up in the first place, perhaps through a better mixture of running and walking and with more regular attention to stretching each time I took a break.

I wondered whether we could cut down on the breaks. Last time we had started at 6am and rested for 20 minutes at lunchtime at around noon, with a 10 minute break at teatime at 4pm and a final 20/30 minute stop for dinner at 7pm. We had finished each day about 11pm. Theoretically this then gave around 7 hours rest. But in practice the time spent off route and with massage and repairs reduced this to under 6 hours per night.

Experience of subsequent multi-day events had suggested that breaks were well worth the time spent. They provided valuable rest for tired muscles and also relief for the mind, especially when we were on main roads and needed some break from the constant traffic. It would be false economy to try to cut down on the total rest for the day. However, if I could be massaged and my feet repaired while I was resting and eating a main meal, then the maximum benefit could be gained from the stop. This might lengthen the lunch and dinner breaks slightly but we might save by cutting out the tea stop.

To synchronise the van movements around mealtimes, so as to ensure that James Tomkies, our medical man, was on the spot during those breaks, would require considerable organisation. Food cannot be cooked on the move because the gas cannot be safely switched on with the vans in motion. So the off-duty van would have to go ahead and do the cooking which would then have to be ready at the precise moment I arrived. But arrived where? How could the crew know exactly where I was going to be? How could they synchronise their movements so precisely and yet have sufficient rest periods? If the crews started to get worn out through charging up and down the roads and not having sufficient rest, they would start to fail in their support tasks and that would inevitably affect me.

One answer was to have mobile phones so that the vans could communicate. But this could not be the complete answer because there could be areas where the reception was poor, especially in hilly country or parts of Scotland. Also it would be no good knowing that the van with my food was stuck in traffic 5 miles back or 5 miles ahead on a dual carriageway and couldn't get to me. Five miles would involve another hour's walking/running. So a detailed schedule would be needed of probable progress each day and for the vans to liaise closely and agree to rendezvous ahead of the likely meal stop.

We then needed to decide how long each van should be on duty and how long scouting the route ahead, shopping, showering and resting.

Our experience of the multi-day Paris-Colmar event, where we used the van on a shift system, suggested that a 6 hour shift was perhaps best. Anything much less and the crews did not seem to get enough rest by the time they had tidied up after their on-duty

100

session, had showers, made themselves a decent meal and then driven ahead to have a rest. Any longer than 6 hours meant that they began to relax too much, lose the close involvement and become bored. Equally, while on duty they could get tired, especially in the heat, and lose the motivation and enthusiasm which ought to be conveyed to the walker on the road.

If one van were to lead off at 6am with the next joining at the lunch stop at noon, that might have been satisfactory. But the first van would then find itself on again at 6pm and hence would then start and finish the day. On that basis its crew would get worn out while the second van would only have one work session.

Somehow we would have to create four roughly equal sessions with one van starting off at dawn and the other taking me through at the end of the day to the night stop. That would mean that the morning van crew would have to remain awake and stop overnight at the same point as the other van that was accompanying me. This would only work if that crew did not remain on duty too long in the morning and could be certain of getting a few hours rest before coming back on duty.

In the event my van crews settled naturally into roughly 4½ hour shift patterns with the crew, to which James Tomkies our medic belonged, being on duty over the lunch stop and waiting for me at the 7pm dinner stop.

Sandra's crews decided they wanted to operate on longer shift patterns of at least 8 hours. While this gave time for the off duty crew to enjoy the countryside and visit some of the sights being passed, it ran the danger both of a loss of focus and of a loss of contact with the other crew. The latter was indeed to happen.

In Doug's view (and admittedly with the benefit of hindsight) "the strong message here is that both vans should always be in close touch to react quickly to changed circumstances, which will always happen on such a long, eventful and potentially stressful event."

Other actions in the detailed programme Doug and I had set were more easily dealt with.

I wrote to Stuart Newport at the Guinness Book of Records with the sheet I proposed to use as a sighting form. The Guinness Book of Records requires first of all, regular sightings along the route from people who can be identified (hence their name and address has to be written down) with the time and place also recorded. Our forms had photographs of us so that people could easily confirm it was us they had seen.

Secondly, Guinness require a signed statement from one member of the crew that we had indeed gone all the way on foot and that if we had left the route (eg, to go to a campsite) that we had rejoined the route at precisely the same spot.

Finally they need some evidence that the person claiming a record has performed similar feats in the past. This is no doubt to avoid a repetition of the situation that existed on the Land's End to John O'Groats for many years, after a certain Fred Hicks had claimed that in May 1977 he had run about 870 miles from Land's End to John O'Groats in 10 days 3 hours and 30 minutes. The route was longer in those days not least because there were no bridges over, for example, the Cromarty Firth. This makes it all the more remarkable if he had indeed travelled such a long distance within the time claimed. The trouble was that he had evidently been supported only by his wife in a caravan. More significantly, he had never been recorded as having done any significant performance in any long distance race before he completed the event, and was never recorded doing anything significant afterwards. His claim was classed as "unauthenticated" and the official record remained that of Don Ritchie.

But there was always, in my mind at least, a nagging question mark as to whether Fred Hicks had in fact done what he had claimed, and hence was the true record holder. My time was to remove that question once and for all.

I copied my correspondence to Andy Milroy, the Road Runners Club statistician, whom I knew would be contacted by the Guinness Book of Records and would make the final recommendation. Just before we started, we received confirmation that all was in order - just as well since both Sandra and I had had about 20 copies of the forms printed.

The route was to some extent fixed already. In July 1980 Geoff Ellingham and Mike Powell-Davies had devised a route for Ann Sayer who in September of that year had set a women's walking record (it was also the foot record since no runner had gone any faster) of 13 days 17 hours 42 minutes. It was an incredibly detailed route description, as might have been expected from Geoff

102

who is a fanatic at precise route planning for the Long Distance Walkers Association and has organised many excellent cross-country events, where navigation and detailed route descriptions are the keys to a successful outing. An example at around the 100 mile point gives some flavour of the overall description:

"Okehampton, 99 miles, A30 cross two bridges, at second junction on left go ahead and slightly left on minor road. In 20 yards join B3215, Belstone Corner 102.5 miles, continue ahead over rail bridge, later ahead on A3072..." and so it goes on.

I had marked Ordnance Survey maps from Land's End to John O'Groats on the basis of this description for the 1988 run and we had followed it religiously.

I now wanted to make some changes. I did not want to go over the hills via Peebles in the Scottish Lowlands. Even though it was a slightly more direct route on the map it had proved very hilly and tiring. I therefore thought that this time we would stay on the main roads via Hawick, Selkirk and Galashiels. The maps suggested that this would be slightly less hilly. In the event I suspect there was nothing in it, especially as we approached Edinburgh from the south east and then had to make a seemingly endless ring-road bypass of the city to get to the Forth Road Bridge some way to the west.

In some other places Doug suggested changes which kept us on main roads (which Ann and Geoff had wanted to avoid where possible in 1980 so as to reduce the mental strains from the endless traffic) which were generally flatter. A lot of energy and time is used in climbing hills and you never get either of them back on the downhill.

Some flexibility to react to the circumstances on the ground is also important. As Doug said, *"The ideal route was the best balance between mileage, gradients, traffic flows, surface and interest. Some of this can be judged from the maps, but sometimes decisions had to be made on site. These would then be relayed back to Sandra's vans."*

Once the route had been confirmed and the detailed maps marked or re-marked, we could set a daily schedule and tell Countrywide which towns we would be passing and roughly when so that an outline media schedule could be prepared and advance information sent off to the various radio and TV stations and newspapers along the route.

The schedule we set was as follows:

Day 1	Okehampton	90 miles
Day 2	Avon border	85 miles
Day 3	Leominster	80 miles
Day 4	South of Warrington	80 miles
Day 5	Kendal	79 miles
Day 6	South of Hawick	79 miles
Day 7	South of Kinross	77 miles
Day 8	Dromochter Pass	78 miles
Day 9	Invergordon	78 miles
Day 10	North of Helmsdale	75 miles
Day 11	John O'Groats	30 miles
		830 miles

This was designed to get us to John O'Groats in around 10½ days. If things went well, we would be up on our schedule in the second half. But if we were to recapture the record, then we could not afford to slip much behind this schedule.

I reckoned that over the first day when I was fresh and when the A30 with its long and fairly gentle gradients had taken much of the sting out of the Cornish and Devon hills, I should be able to do 90 miles without over-tiring myself. We could then have a good rest. It would be so tempting to press on and even go through the first night without sleep. But this was not a 24 or 48 hour event and had to be approached differently. The distance and time had to be respected and the pace planned appropriately.

I remember Malcolm Campbell saying over his gin and tonic in the Grantham pub that you just had to think of a multi-day event as being just like any other day; only instead of getting up and going to work, you got up and went out on the road. You broke for lunch and dinner and then at bedtime relaxed, showered and got a good night's sleep before starting the same routine again the next day.

Eighty-five miles on the second day would allow a taper down in distance as the running element reduced. It would however be sufficient to take us up the first range of hills south of Bristol. We could then start the third day at the top of the hill and warm up by running down. Eighty miles on day 3 would take us to our first free hotel stop in Leominster just as the pubs were closing.

I had decided to go via the Wye Valley rather than the flat Gloucester plain because although there was not much in it in distance, the Wye Valley route with its wonderful views of Tintern Abbey would be more inspiring than the views of Oldbury Nuclear Power Station.

For the remaining days we would then average just over three marathons a day to come home in about 10½ days. If things went well or badly we always had the opportunity to go through the last night with short snatches of sleep and either improve on the schedule or catch back some lost time if we had fallen behind.

Since we could not afford to get lost or waste any time going through towns, Doug sent off for town maps for every town on the route. He then measured the options and marked with a yellow marker pen the precise route that we would take. In some cases, one-way streets meant that the vans would go a different route. In other cases, I could cut through pedestrian precincts. We became neurotic about the few yards I might save or waste, and the need for utter certainty on the route.

I must have driven Doug mad even before we started, but the spectre of those lost few minutes here and there last time round haunted me, and I was convinced that if we were to break the record, the margin for error would be very small indeed. Neither did I want the mental aggro on the event of worrying whether we were taking the best route. I needed the certainty that everything had been planned and that everything was going precisely as it should be so that all I had to do was just keep putting one foot in front of the other.

As it happened, the navigation through every town was superb. A member of the team (often Doug himself), with map in hand, would walk or jog with me while the van would usually be just a few yards ahead and signalling at junctions which way we had to go. Sometimes we had two crew members on the road with one holding up traffic so I could make the shortest route round (or over!) roundabouts or across busy roads.

Interestingly, it was on side roads where I think we made four errors each of which cost no more than about 5 minutes. One of them seemed as much the fault of the map as the navigator, and on another occasion a new bit of road had been built which was not on the map.

Our route schedule fixed, we turned to food and drink. Sandra and I each wrote out our preferences and Doug's wife Jill descended on the Bristol supermarkets and loaded down her Landrover Discovery with enough food and drink to keep all four vans going for the first two days. The list of food is an Appendix.

There is an emphasis on carbohydrate, the essential basis of the body's glycogen fuel that will feed our muscles. Research has shown the importance of continuous intakes of carbohydrate with as much as 80% of food intake being in this form on an ultra event. Even for normal healthy living, some 70% might be carbohydrate, with 15-20% protein and 15-20% fat. Most people (including some athletes) eat too much fat while others still eat unnecessarily large amounts of protein. Only if you are building muscle or working at high intensity levels so that you are destroying muscle cells do you need more than 15% protein.

In any activity, the muscles will first call upon the glycogen stored locally around those muscles. As this begins to get used, so the body will call upon the glycogen stored in the liver. Carbo-loading before an event seeks to maximise the amount of glycogen stored in the body, which can then readily be called upon and used by the muscles. As the liver glycogen is reduced, so the body will call upon carbohydrate which it will convert into glycogen. It will also start to break down fats stored in the body, but this process will take much longer.

If the muscles are used too hard, the readily available glycogen will be used and the body might not have had the opportunity to convert enough carbohydrates or fats into usable energy. In that case the muscles will soon tire and the body will "hit the wall".

Quality training aims in part to push out the time it takes to hit the wall by improving metabolic conversion rates. It will also increase the amount of glycogen which can be stored, not least by raising the number of minute blood-carrying veins (micondria) around the main muscle groupings. These will also remove the lactic acid waste by-products of muscular activity which can be another cause of wall hitting. If the veins become too full of lactic acid, the muscles will be starved of oxygen just as they are starved

106

of glycogen and hence will cease to operate efficiently. They will do the same if they become overheated or are too cold.

If the carbohydrate intake is inadequate to meet the body's needs, then, given the time it takes to convert fat into fuel, there is the danger that the muscles could start to feed on protein, convert this into carbohydrate, and literally start to feed on itself and eat itself away. Sir Ranulph Fiennes, in his book on crossing Antarctica, describes how he lost not only about a third of total body weight but even more of muscle mass. Admittedly, he and his colleague were much heavier than us to start with (having to pull sledges across Antarctica rather than run across it) but with our low body fat contents, there was a real danger that any loss of weight would reflect a loss of muscle mass and hence slow us.

For someone walking 25 miles a day carrying a certain amount of spare fat (Ian Botham and his Land's End to John O'Groats walk somehow happens to come into my mind!) the chance of muscle depletion would be much less than for someone such as myself with a body fat content of only 8% to start with and who is then running and walking over 80 miles a day.

To help minimise the loss of protein, I decided to try to ensure not only that I ate enough protein in the form of eggs for breakfast, tuna sandwiches as one of my snacks plus protein for lunch and dinner, but also to take protein supplements in the form of amino-acids. These are the basic building blocks of life, the basis from which protein is made. In tablet form they are easy to take. I hope they helped. If they did me no good, they certainly did me no harm.

The same would be true of the vitamin and mineral supplements I took every 6 hours. Finally I needed my anti-inflammatory Naproxen back tablets for the ankylosing spondilitis I have suffered since my late teens. I hoped I would not sound like a drug bottle rattling along the road. But I felt it important that we took these tablets regularly.

I therefore drew up a schedule for every half hour of every day on which the crews had to confirm that they had given me some food and drink with my tablet collection every 6 hours. Experience has shown that it is often difficult to be certain when you have eaten while on a long-distance event. It is so easy for the time to pass and in the excitement of approaching a checkpoint or catching another competitor or going through a town to forget. You can end up going for an hour without proper carbohydrate intake. But unless the energy expenditure can be roughly matched by energy intake, the energy difference has to be made up from within the body itself. If the deficiency becomes too great then you quickly lose momentum and physical tiredness converts itself into mental tiredness.

In 1992 Sandra was lying just some 20 minutes behind the leader of the women's event in the Paris-Colmar as she started to climb the long Col du Bonhomme. Concentrating on the task of closing the gap by the top and misjudging or mismemorising the length of the ascent, she only drank a weak isostar solution on the hour-long climb. Her crew failed to insist on her eating, and although she closed a few minutes she was visibly tiring by the top. Once over the col and into an upward current of north-facing cold wind, she nearly collapsed, had to be wrapped in blankets and coats, and given warm drinks and constant attention. She dropped over an hour behind the leader in the last 20 miles.

If you wait until you feel hungry, it is too late. Similarly, on a hot day if you wait until you feel thirsty before you drink, you are already dehydrated and will remain so.

I am glad to say that the drink/food/tablet schedule was rigorously followed by my crews. Sandra seemed less certain that she was getting all the food she needed at regular intervals. Maybe if she had had a similar schedule, her crews could have been more certain what was being consumed and when.

A normal day's diet is totally inadequate for any long-distance event or even a long day's walk in the hills. I remember Bruce Tulloh saying that an all-day 25 mile cross-country walk over the hills required double portions of everything at dinner time to replace the number of calories consumed. Maybe that is one reason why we do these ultra events; so we can really carbo load beforehand and tuck in afterwards. We have less need to worry about the volume we eat and certainly enjoy our food at every mealtime.

We do however care about and monitor closely what we eat. No butter, cream, cheese, red meats or biscuits will generally pass our lips. Vegetables, fruits, bread, pasta, fish, pulses, yoghurts and fruit juices (and the occasional beer and wine!) are the order of the day. If ever I get withdrawal symptoms for some good local cheddar cheese offered at a luncheon or dinner, weaken and take a corner, I always feel I have to work that little bit longer at the next day's training session.

If this seems unnecessarily hair-shirtish, I would respond by saying that there is a fine line between being a champion and a record holder and just being the person that always comes second or third. That line might be determined by the extra quality of the training, by that extra bit of mental training and determination on the day, or it might be the 1% difference in fat content and hence "excess" body weight that someone is carrying around because the optimum diet has not been followed. What is the point in training in all weathers and going through mental visualisation and stimulation sessions if you then knock back a few pints of beer and a bag of crisps?

If you are aiming for the top, you have to get it right in all you do all of the time. The margin for error does not allow any other approach.

Achieving success in whatever we have chosen requires self discipline and a wholehearted commitment. As you start to live and breathe that new way of life, so it becomes in-built and second nature. It becomes natural to get up early and exercise, to cut down on the fatty foods and to look forward to the next challenge. The new cycle of life becomes a virtuous circle of doing the right things and thinking the right thoughts more and more of the time. You start living the life you want to live.

It is not a struggle to achieve your vision. It slowly becomes your way of life. You wonder why you did not follow this pattern before. You certainly would not now want to lead any different life.

I hope the following lessons have emerged:

Plan everything down to the finest detail wherever you can. Leave nothing to chance.

Simulate as much as you can what has to be done and work through systematically to see that everything has been covered. Think through how it will actually feel on the day. Options and fall back positions need to have been thought about.

A flexible response to changing circumstances should be accepted and built in, but crisis management should be avoided.

Nutrition, rest and exercise are important keys to a successful long life, as well as any adventure. Getting the balance right and attending to the details of each will make the difference between an average and a winning performance whatever the objective in life.

If we are focused and really committed to achieve our goals, then our whole way of life will slowly adapt to meet the objectives we have set. We will naturally ease ourselves into new routines and thought patterns and build confidence as we live our new life on our terms.

10

Land's End to the Mendips

The Land's End complex is an interesting collection of white-painted buildings clustered round a hotel perched above the cliffs. The hotel's dining room must have one of the best views in Britain, particularly when the sun sets over the rolling Atlantic and you imagine the vast expanse of ocean between you and the North American coast.

There are exhibitions on local Cornish life and history in the neighbouring buildings, with stories about the tin-miners, the ship-wreckers and some of the local personalities. Sandra and I were particularly interested in the story of another great long distance walk undertaken by an 85 year old Newlyn fishwife.

In August 1851, Mary Kelynack (who had been born in Madron in 1766) decided she would walk to London to see the Great Exhibition. She was used to walking to Truro and reasoned that London couldn't be much further. Her walk became famous and hundreds turned up at the roadside as she strode determinedly towards the capital. On 24th September 1851, five weeks after setting off from Penzance, she arrived in the capital. She walked to the Mansion House and asked to see the Lord Mayor. Later she met Queen Victoria and Prince Albert, the former describing her as 'the most famous woman in England.' About the end of September she set off for Penzance once more and eventually arrived home safely. She died on 5th December 1855 at the ripe age of 89.

I wondered what clothes she had worn. Had the craze for "bloomers" reached West Cornwall?

The introduction of Mrs Amelia Bloomer's controversial costume of coatee or bodice, short skirt and under it pantaloons or "bloomers" reaching to the ankles made athletic exercise more feasible for women than it was in crinolines. Mrs Bloomer visited

England in 1851, so theoretically it was possible that Mary Kelynack had caught the craze. My father wore his first pair of jeans when he was 80; so why not bloomers at 85! Mary Kelynack is buried in the local churchyard. Sandra read the story with particular interest, on the evening of 4th May, the day before we started our adventure.

In a nearby field stands a circle of large stones - maidens enticed by the Devil to dance in an ever more demented manner through Saturday night and into the Sabbath. There would be no overnight dancing for us.

Just a few miles away on the south coast lies Mousehole. This charming stone-built fishing port has been the inspiration for many a children's picture-book as the terrifying storm cat tries to get in through the tight entrance to the harbour, fails in his attempt and is eventually tamed by Tom and his singing cat as they venture forth to catch the ling for their fish stew and sardines for their stargazy pie.

Less romantically, one of Sandra's crews opened a tin of tuna by the roadside and brewed up tea on the way down. The rest of us piled into Admiral Benbow's restaurant in the old centre of Penzance.

This pub has a restaurant area at the back like a below-deck stern of a sailing ship with portholes, tackle and lamps swinging. It creates a suitable nautical atmosphere especially when a large party of adventurers descend on the galley. The food turned out to be very good and reasonable and the whole evening was an excellent pre-race get together.

We walked through the quiet streets of Penzance after our meal savouring the smells of the sea, the calm of the evening and the anticipation of the days to come. Everything we could think of had been planned and we could not think of anything last minute to panic about. Like commanders before a battle, Doug, Sandra and I walked quietly back to the line of parked vans on the quayside. They looked as though they were in battle formation and raring to go. They also seemed to have a quality of Thomas the Tank Engine and his friends. I could imagine them talking to each other while we were having our dinner, comparing notes on their experiences and asking each other if they knew what was in store and what new adventure they were about to embark on.

112

They moved off quietly and drove the last few miles to Lands End where they huddled together in the car park looking out to sea. Their lights went out and all was calm.

At 5.30 am on 5 May the sun had yet to burn off the early morning mist but an easterly breeze was stirring. The flags were fluttering at the entrance to the cluster of white painted buildings and a few seagulls strutted hopefully around the doors of the hotel. As there was no sign of life, they took off to investigate the unexpected activity in the neighbouring car park.

There, our four camper vans were a hive of activity. The lights were on inside and silhouettes could be seen jostling for room in the restricted space to store sleeping bags, put on jumpers or down an early morning cup of tea.

Don Thompson had decided to sleep out in his sleeping bag under the stars. As the east wind picked up in the middle of the night he got increasingly cold, but kindly chose not to clamber into the van for comfort as that would have disturbed our last decent night's sleep for ten days. His cheery face now appeared at the window and we let him in for a warming mug of tea.

Outside, darker figures grouped round a mountain bike which had just been taken down from the rack protruding from the largest van. Two others were attempting to stick a large banner on the back of a van. The breeze had a go at taking the banner across the car park, but eventually it was held in place by thick, green tape. The lights of a third van picked out the large letters: *"The Gump Run. World Record Attempt Land's End to John O'Groats, Thank You for Waiting".*

Mr Motivator had made some fairly good predictions when he set the scene with us on GMTV:

"Those of you worrying about whether you will complete your first marathon, spare a thought for the couple who aim to run three marathons a day every day for ten days. During that time they will each day use up five thousand calories, drink twelve pints of water, wear five pairs of trainers and make three changes of clothes .... *and use a lot of blister pads".*

As before every event, Sandra and I focused on getting ready for the off. We went through our routines of dressing the feet and deciding how many layers of clothes to put on.

We relaxed with deep breathing and tried not to get caught up

113

in the rush of adrenalin which started to affect every member of the team. "At last the great day has arrived, how do you feel? OK? Want another slice of toast? What about this anti-chafing cream; have you got enough on?" We retreated still further into ourselves to gain peace. After a few minutes we decided to go to the hotel to put our names in the book of the Lands End to John O'Groats Society and get a form stamped. They were just opening the hotel and a middle-aged lady at reception went through the motions of stamping the form as though this was some chore she had to do every morning around this time. Maybe it was. They say that in the height of the season, up to twenty hopefuls start off each day on foot, bicycle, car or other forms of transport to make the attempt to John O'Groats. I wonder how many make it.

The lad behind the bar cleaning the coffee cups was more chatty and enthusiastic. He wished us well and looked as though he meant it.

We went in search of the post which all end-to-enders touch in hopefulness at the start or exhaustion at the finish. It had the mileage to John O'Groats as 874. We preferred our 830 miles estimate. There was just time to put the letters Gump Run 5th May on the sign before my watch blipped to tell me it was 6 am. We took off a layer of clothing and at 6.01 am set off towards the ball of fire that was just rising over the inland hills.

Our crews were hardly prepared for our departure and there was a great scurrying around the vans and running across the car park to take pictures and wave us off.

Then all was peace for a few moments as we jogged gently over the little hill on which sits the village of Sennen. Needless to say, there is an inn called the "First and Last". We passed this after another pub, so presumably it wasn't! Or maybe there is a subtle difference between an inn and a pub. Also, the inn was in an old stone building and had clearly been there longer. We decided it deserved the title.

After a mile or so we could hear one of our support vans closing on us. The slamming of a door and noise of feet was followed by the offer of a drink from one of our cycling water bottles. After another couple of miles more feet brought an offer of a marmalade sandwich. We knew the crews were already settling into the routine that should be their pattern for the next ten days.

By the time we had jogged the ten miles to Penzance, the ball of fire was getting high and very hot. We both had on our broad-rimmed peaked caps and Sandra was applying sun tan lotion. "Do we have any lotion?" I asked Debbie who was by now cycling alongside me. With a nifty U-turn she went back to the van. It appeared we didn't have any. So Doug decided to give Debbie enough food and drink to last me for the next hour while he took the van into Penzance. He needed to fill up with petrol in any event.

I pinched some of Sandra's cream and we started up the A30 towards the old fishing port of Hayle which is interestingly on the north rather than on the south coast. The A30 bypasses this village, but on the map it looked just as short and probably more pleasant to go on the old road.

We had started to walk up the long dual carriageway incline out of Penzance. Sandra seemed to want to walk at a faster pace than me, so I let her go. It is important to go at your own pace and do your own thing. And I certainly was not going to push it too hard in the heat of the day.

By the time we reached Hayle she was a quarter of a mile ahead and staying on the bypass. "Oh well, perhaps she can't be bothered to take the scenic route," I thought. In fact, neither she nor her crew were aware of the preferred route we had plotted. It was an omen for worse navigational errors which were to happen later.

I had memorised most of each day's route particularly where there were deviations. Being so closely involved in the detailed route planning and decisions on the options had undoubtedly helped. Sandra was more reliant on her crew to get it right.

In practice the Hayle option made no difference. I walked on the flat through the village whilst Sandra walked up the detour and down the other side to cross my path the same distance ahead as she had been. I fell in line again a quarter of a mile behind.

The area around Camborne is littered with the ruins of old mine buildings with their tall stone chimneys. You can imagine the great Thomas Trevithick and George Watt beam engines now in the Science Museum and Kew Pumping Station in London slowly pumping water from the shafts and no doubt forcing air down others. The ruins have a solidity even in their roofless state and stand proud amongst the heather and gorse.

You have the feeling that this was where the Industrial Revolution started. Not in the dark satanic mills of the north, but here in the windswept open moorland. It was here where tin has been mined from time immemorial and where the Phoenicians were reputed to have sailed to from the Mediterranean before the Romans came. From here ancient paths still fan out across Salisbury Plain to the Icknield Way and the Norfolk Flint Mines in an ancient two-way trade with tin going one way and the flints needed to hack it out of the rocks travelling back the other.

I felt like one of our ancient forebears moving on foot as they would have done across a landscape which in this part of the country may not have changed much. The great woods of southern England destroyed for timber for the Navy and for charcoal and other uses, would probably not have covered this bleak upland area.

I jogged on down one of the long inclines on the A30 and slowly caught Sandra. She was walking faster up the hills but was not able to run with such a long stride down them. I wondered what her plan was. We had not discussed her ideas but I had a sense that she and Boyd Millen had worked out some scheme. She was well capable of getting to John O'Groats before me if she repeated her consistent "clockwork doll" pattern with minimum sleep which had seen her complete the Gibson Ranch Six-Day Race so successfully.

I had my pre-arranged pattern of walking up the hills and running down them and I was not going to be tempted to match what Sandra was doing. It was not a race and we were not competing against each other. The object was to get to John O'Groats faster than anyone had ever done it before and for me that meant keeping to the schedule we had carefully established.

I remembered the quotation from an "Indianapolis 500" rally driver:
"To finish first, you must first finish."
I told myself:
"We don't need to go any faster, especially not in this heat. I must not wear myself out on the first day. If we have to go slower than

116

intended then so be it; the objective is what matters; we can always catch up later when the weather cools".

The sun was now so hot that I was using sunblock lotion every hour and drinking what seemed like pints of water and carbohydrate drink every few minutes. We had chosen early May for the run to coincide with the release on video of the film Forrest Gump but we also thought it would be a pleasant time of year. The spring flowers would be out and we hoped there would be some warmth in the sun. But here we had an incredible heatwave.

When the A30 descended into a valley and we lost the cooling easterly breeze, it was like being in a Canyon in the Arizona Dessert. Debbie kept passing me the water bottle so she rode alongside. She was in a bikini top - which she filled fairly amply to the enjoyment of many we passed - and short shorts - which again did not leave a great deal to the imagination of motorists coming up behind.

I had slightly less sex appeal, especially as the white sun tan lotion was so liberally applied that it gave a skeleton-like quality to my arms and shoulders in particular. Doug was much more the part. His bronzed heavy frame was stripped to the waste and he had on a pair of shorts at least as skimpy as Debbie's; with wrap around non-reflective sunglasses and a peaked cap sitting on top of his square face and shoulders, he looked like a tank commander in Rommel's Africa Korps guiding his tank crews in pursuit of the objective. Debbie said he was just a poser but then who was talking!

Whether it was the sight of Debbie or Doug which caused the crash we shall never know. But a van which had been resting in a layby on the other side of the road suddenly woke up, revved out of the layby and did a U-turn to follow us right in front of a car coming up the hill behind. There was a squealing of brakes and that momentary silence you get before the sound of smashed glass. I just said to Debbie "Keep going and don't look back. Doug will sort it". No doubt he did as we heard nothing more.

Our first navigational error occurred just before Launceston. The A30 made a detour and our preferred old path veered left. Amos and his crew were now on duty but at the crucial moment all three of them were in the van and no one was out to shout at me.

I had forgotten exactly where the turning was and kept to the main road instead of veering left. Amos caught me up and we consulted the map while on the move. We went to the next turning and only lost about five minutes. But it was annoying. In future, we always had someone at any turning to make certain we all took the right path.

Sandra was still somewhere ahead as we threaded our way through the Launceston shoppers, across a pedestrian precinct and up the hill out of the town. At the top we saw Sandra and her van joining the route from a different direction. They had obviously done something wrong in the one-way system. Rather selfishly, I felt slightly better and forgot we had gone wrong only a few minutes earlier.

By the time night fell, we were well on our way to Okehampton. Doug phoned ahead to a camp site just outside the town because he wanted to plug his limping van into a power point. Every time he stopped he and his crew had to push start the creature. They had had to make certain that when they needed petrol they found a petrol station on a hill facing the right way.

I only learnt about another inconvenience later. As we were about to leave Bristol to travel to Land's End, Countrywide Communications had communicated to us that we would not have the communications they had undertook to provide. In other words, we had only one mobile phone between the four vans. With all the other pressures on him, Doug had somehow put together a deal and three more phones had miraculously appeared just as the van engines were being started. We could not have survived without them ... or Doug.

The camp site was not open, but the owner kindly agreed to make the showers, the field and the electricity available to us. While Doug went off, Amos closed up right behind me on the busy dual carriageway so his headlights could illuminate me and any potholes ahead. He then put on some music which played through loudspeakers we had fixed facing forward on the outside of the vans. I had found this both highly motivating and at other times relaxing on the Paris - Colmar and it certainly wiled away the hours. To the tunes of Handel's Water Music and Royal Fireworks Suite we marched into the night .... until a blue flashing light added to our illuminations.

The friendly Devon Constabulary in their souped-up Sierra, decided the van was rather dangerous going along at five miles per hour even with its flashing warning lights. Neither were they certain about the music - Philistines! The fact that without the van I would be exposed on the open road with the only illumination coming from a bicycle lamp seemed not to concern them. They sped off into the darkness and Amos went ahead to the next layby.

When I caught up we calculated we had done just over 89 miles. The layby had an AA emergency number box in it and there was a flyover just ahead. So we could easily recognise it in the morning when we returned. We decided to leave the field of battle and join Doug in the showers. We also had to try and recharge the batteries in Doug's run down charabanc and try and make it a roadworthy campervan.

Some miles back I had finally caught Sandra on a downhill stretch and walked with her on a pleasant old road through the bracken and gorse and across a pack horse bridge. Where this old road came next to the new one there was now a wooden fence and motorway-style barriers. Derek was on the bike and he went ahead to spy-out the land. He had not returned by the time I reached the fence so I climbed over, crossed the barriers, ran across the dual carriageway and over the intermediate barriers to resume my progress on the left-hand side of the main road. Sandra declined the gate vault and kept to the old road, presumably also telling Derek where I had gone. The old road rejoined later on and after a few minutes a tired and hot Derek eventually caught me with a large bottle of drink.

Sandra was therefore now somewhere behind us in the dark as we sped off for our welcome shower. I wondered where she would stop for the night.

The camp site was indeed not open. The grass was three feet high and there were sheep in the field. Don Thompson decided he would take his sleeping bag into the owner's front garden away from the sheep. And so at midnight all was quiet. We had done virtually 90 miles as we had planned at a steady pace in unexpected heat into a slight headwind. We could feel pleased with the first day's efforts.

At 4.30 in the morning, there was a hurried entry into the van by Don. It was just about time to get moving in any case, but I

119

was surprised by Don's agility so early. It soon transpired that he had been woken a few moments earlier by the friendly licking of a large Doberman dog in the owner's garden where he had chosen to pitch his sleeping bag for the night. Although apparently still in one piece and none the worse for the experience, he had nevertheless retreated rather fast to seek sanctuary in our van. He was never again to sleep under the stars during our journey!

We packed the sleeping bags away and Doug unplugged the mains from the battery recharger. He switched on the ignition and all the lights dimmed. He had forgotten to trip the master recharge switch. All our detour and efforts to give new life to his battery had been in vain. We cursed the vehicle hire company still louder.

Amos hurriedly started his engine and drew nose to nose; so hurriedly that he completely forgot to unplug his recharger. Fortunately, there was no loud bang, just a broken plug and more cursing.

By the time we had started the van, found our way out of the three feet high grass field without mowing down any sheep, back to the A30 and up to our start point, it was 5.30 am. Not good enough. We had to get Doug's van repaired and keep to our plan of sleeping on the route.

After half-an-hour's walking during which I enjoyed a bowl of Weetabix, some scrambled egg and bread and a mug of tea, we passed one of Sandra's vans in a layby. It was completely quiet with the curtains drawn. We did not disturb them. Obviously, Sandra had continued walking way beyond the time when we stopped, had effectively overtaken us in the night (although she may not have realised that since our vans had left the route) and was now some way ahead.

Well passed Okehampton we saw her walking up a hill with Boyd Millen. As we approached we could also see she had her arms down by her side rather than up in brisk race walking style. She was also going fairly slowly compared with how she had been the day before. Her crew told us she had been affected badly by the heat and had suffered with diarrhoea. She had kept going rather than rest and had had just one-and-half-hour's sleep. Now she was trying to consolidate her stomach while taking it steady. Her feet had also swollen in the heat and that had resulted in some rubbing and hence blistering around the heels. This was not good news after just one day.

I passed some words of encouragement to her and gave her a morning kiss, but there was no point in walking with her. Better for her to walk within herself and slowly get everything back together again. If she took it steady, I was sure she would be OK. We had both had stomach problems on many events and lived to tell the tale. Boyd also had a variety of potions and pills and I knew she was in good hands.

Doug had at last got the van mechanics to replace both alternator and battery. Maybe the hassle he and his crew had had to endure would now be at an end. It would be a great relief to them. I had largely been shielded from the aggro but I realised it must have been a real pain especially at the start of an event when everyone is naturally a bit on edge and the team has yet to settle down. The last thing you need is some major problem not of your making with the van.

Doug immediately phoned Amos to tell him the good news. He used the redial button to be clever, and the mechanic's phone rang five yards away!

South of Taunton we made another navigational error on minor roads and this time, since we were going in the wrong direction, I jumped into the van to be taken back to where we had gone off route.

It was however wonderful to be off the main A30 and able to enjoy the peaceful country lanes. The overhanging trees offered the occasional shade and the spring flowers were out in glorious profusion. I thought of my colleagues at work in their sealed office and even more so of London commuters fighting on the underground in a large sweaty mass. I knew where I would rather be.

As we passed through Taunton a young man in an open-top BMW made a suitable gesture with a clenched fist and erect arm as Debbie cycled past. This drew the response from me "leave her alone, she's mine" and the equally fast response from Debbie "not until the finish". Since Debbie wasn't going to the finish but had to get the train back from Preston, that did not give me as great an encouragement as it might have done.

As we neared the dinner-time change over point, Angela Dudley and a colleague from Sparks appeared with great banners for the sides of the vans. These gave the 0891 number which people could phone to hear a recorded message from Sally Gunnell and how they could enter a competition to win a state-of-the-art TV and video recorder. After they had tied the banners on, they set off with collecting buckets to knock at neighbouring doors. Cyril joked to them about squeezing the poor (we were parked in the less salubrious part of Bridgwater for dinner) but they seemed reluctant to do the pub and restaurant circuit even though I am sure their charm would have got them some full buckets of coins.

As we moved off after enjoying a pasta, tuna and vegetable main course followed by banana custard, I remembered that in 1988 we had also stopped in Bridgwater for dinner. So we were exactly on schedule for our 85 miles on the second day. Refreshed and encouraged, despite the heat, we were in good shape and going well as I set off along the Somerset levels to the silhouette of the Mendip Hills and the Avon border.

As darkness fell, we passed a sign for Sedgemoor District Council by an old stone bridge over one of the dykes. I recalled how the Duke of Monmouth's rural volunteers had attempted to surprise the trained troops of King James II in 1688 where they had camped in this area. Failing to get across a dyke which barred their way, their noise had alerted an outpost which promptly gave the alarm. In the ensuing confusion, Monmouth's cavalry charged up and down the dyke only succeeding in frightening their own ammunition baggage train. The result was that Monmouth's cannon soon ran out of shot leaving the King's artillery to play havoc with the volunteer force facing them. In the gloom of the evening and with a slight mist rising, the picture of a dawn slaughter in the low-lying land around us was all too real. The very name Sedgemoor seemed so aptly to conjure up the area.

The scurrying of feet brought Jill Green, one of Sandra's van leaders alongside. She had just come off duty but was in her England shorts and proceeded to race walk at a fast pace alongside while giving me the latest news from Sandra. Evidently her stomach had now stabilized and she was feeling much better. Taking on solids she had regained her strength and was walking well. Her feet, however, continued to give her trouble especially in the heat and they were too painful to run on. She was, however, in good spirits and sent her love.

I was pleased that Sandra was in better shape though a bit disturbed about her feet. Three weeks earlier in the first of the race walking internationals in France we had both suffered. It had rained for the first twelve hours and my feet were blistered as a result. The rain softens and wrinkles skin and removes the creams which aim to stop them rubbing against the shoes. Plasters which cover known sensitive or dangerous spots also become wrinkled and move around causing more problems than they are worth. Soon large blistered areas develop and short of continually stopping to repair the damage and change socks and shoes for dry pairs (a waste of time when the water is running like streams down the roads) you just have to press on.

Around 100 miles, I had called it a day. I had had a good long training outing, was in about eighth position, which was quite respectable, and saw no purpose in pushing on just to finish if that would damage my heels still further. The objective was a record-breaking Lands End to John O'Groats and I could not afford to knock myself about too much in a race that was just a training milestone along the schedule I had set myself.

Sandra meanwhile was engaged in a battle with the winner of the previous year's Paris-Colmar women's race - Joelle Lefilleuil. Joelle's support crew were out pacing her and spurring her on and Sandra was not prepared to concede victory to her just because her feet were hurting.

She eventually completed over 189km in the 24 hours to beat Joelle convincingly by about 6km and win the ladies' race. I now wondered, however, whether her feet had really recovered. The blisters on her heels had been very deep and probably could not have repaired themselves in three weeks. Still if they got no worse, she would be able to keep to race walking and perhaps be able to jog down a few hills later on. I hoped so.

Jill asked how I was feeling and remarked on my fast walking pace. "You're certainly speeding along. Faster than Sandra. I can only just keep up". I did not like to let on that I had been going slower and had only speeded up when she came alongside and proceeded to drag me along at her faster pace. I said I felt fine with no problems and sent my love back down the line to Sandra.

The injection of additional pace had in fact provided a new momentum, while Jill's encouragement and her good news on

Sandra also spurred me on. There is always a danger in any task that you get into a bit of a rut, a routine which is fine in its way but which can result in your slowly and imperceptibly losing the momentum. You need a sudden stimulus to jolt you out of lethargy or complacency or just the plain tedium of doing a repetitive task. That is one reason why the Swedish approach to building a car with teams rather than via standard American style production lines with its repetitive tasks, held such a fascination. People can give more if the job is more varied and they have greater control and responsibility.

Jill left and the noise of her van receded.

The dark outline of the Mendips against the slightly lighter evening sky beckoned us. The hills slowly grew in height as we approached until they loomed over us. It seemed as though we had to walk right into them and be enveloped by their tree-lined cloaks. After the Somerset Levels, the height of the Mendips was exaggerated and they took on an ancient primeval quality. Mother Earth was about to embrace us.

Then the illusion was shattered as the headlights from a car came down her flanks revealing the way we must go.

It would be a steep climb but there was no point in slowing up. It was already 11 o'clock and I wanted to make it to the top over the Avon border and achieve our 85 mile objective before we turned in for the night. So reinforced with some carbohydrate drink, I led the way with Derek carrying further drinks and illuminating the reflective flashes on my gear with his torch. We strode up the hill to turn off into an excellent parking place right at the summit. The vans were there side by side looking welcoming with their interior lights on. I hauled myself into Doug's van and enjoyed a hot shower before James got to work with a relaxing massage. My feet were a bit swollen but in pretty good shape. Another good day.

I suggested we started at 4.30 pm. Doug told Amos, and after James had finished the massage, he turned out the lights at just past midnight.

Some thoughts on the first stage:

124

Do your own thing. If you have a well rehearsed plan which has been thoroughly thought through, then keep to it. Have the confidence not to be distracted.

Focus on the job in hand. It is sometimes easy to be distracted. That is when errors occur and when the momentum can be lost.

If things do go a bit wrong, do not worry. Just get back on course, refocus, learn from the error so that hopefully it is not repeated and get on with the task you started with renewed vigour.

Adopt a positive stance to everything. Think how much has been accomplished, not how much there is still to do. Take pleasure from the effort and the enjoyment and surprise yourself by how well you are doing.

Use your targets as welcome milestones along your route (whatever the task in hand), and as positive pointers to the future, not as crutches to hold you up.

Set a clear target for the end of each phase and make certain you reach it. Do not compromise and fall short and think you can make it up the following day. The satisfaction of achievement is key to sustaining the winning experience.

11

Across Wales in One-and-a-Half Days

It's good to wake just as it is getting light. The birds are in full chorus, a pair of tawny owls are still hooting, there is much scuttling both in the undergrowth and above you in the trees which have a slightly damp freshness in their Spring greenery. You feel all of nature is just stirring ready for a new day.

I sing inside myself:
"Morning has broken like the first morning,
Blackbird has spoken like the first bird
Praise for the singing
Praise for the morning
Praise for them springing
Fresh from the word."

It was good to start here in the woods at the top of the hill. It had been well worth making the effort the previous evening. It was now downhill all the way ... well at least for the next few miles.

I managed a distinct spring in my step as we set off at a good running pace above the mist, which was lying in the valleys along our way.

The road to Bristol through the outlying hills of the Mendip Ridge is pleasantly undulating. Ian made breakfast as Don and I jogged down the hills to Churchill.

Don was not supposed to be on duty, but as he always got up for a training run at around 4.30 am, he decided to join me. With drinks bottle in hand he nattered away on anything and everything while the fields and trees floated by.

After about an hour we reminded him that it was uphill on the way back to Amos' van. "Oh dear, yes, and Amos doesn't know where I've gone. He'll get annoyed if I'm not around, I'd better get back right away". Don's fear of Amos's wrath suggested the ex-bodyguard of Harold Wilson was ruling his van with an iron will. Don gave one of his ear-to-ear Cheshire cat grins which stayed with me as the rest of him scuttled off back up the hills.

Just south of Bristol on an exposed ridge lies Bristol Airport. It was evidently built there in the Second World War so bomber crews could get practice at bad weather flying. Now it is a fast growing charter and business airport serving the West of England. Its runway has an interesting hill in it so that planes landing from the West hide behind it before rearing up and making their way to the terminal. Those taking off to the West similarly disappear from view just when you expect them to be taking off. It is all a bit disconcerting.

It was as we climbed up to the airport that my Welsh Back training partner, John, joined us. He had motored over from near Axbridge, put his bike in the back of one of the vans and now jogged alongside.

Having a training partner is one way to help maintain the discipline of regular training sessions. If you don't feel like getting up at 6.30 am one cold morning, you have only to think of your partner waiting for you to give you a sense of guilt and get you out of bed. The feeling of not wanting to let someone else down is remarkably powerful.

On regular runs, a partner not only provides company but also motivation. I would not have run so often in all weather through the winter if John had not been there to spur me on. I suspect the same was true for him, as he prepared for the Paris marathon in April.

Neither would I have gone so hard on our training runs. John would time every session we did. He would shout out the time at the top of a long climb out of Bristol to Clifton Heights. As the number of sessions increased, so our times slowly improved.

We would canter over Clifton Suspension Bridge in the gloom of winter, then as dawn was arising behind us and finally as spring turns the trees in the Avon Gorge a glorious fresh green. Having variety in your training, some inspiration and also a feeling that you are slowly improving can get you into a virtuous circle.

From being delighted to have got our times for the longer circuit down to under 1 hour, we became disappointed and held an inquest if we slipped beyond 56 minutes! The improvement was measurable and exhilarating. We knew we were getting fitter and stronger. Our confidence, as a result, increased with each run. It was thanks to John and his encouragement and determination always to do better, that I was able to run so much more on the Forrest Gump Run than I had been able to back in 1988.

I averaged around 70 miles per week during the winter, including gym sessions. This was what I had averaged in previous years. In the summer months the mileage would increase to around 100 miles per week. Beyond 120 miles, studies have suggested the risks of injury and mental and physical fatigue really mount with no net gain to the athlete.

Sandra meanwhile cycled around the clock twice on her exercise bike in London with early morning sessions and the occasional evening workout, after our daughter Victoria had gone to bed. She also had a set of weights (which Victoria seemed rather more proficient at heaving around!).

Every weekend, Sandra would put in at least one long run and return recounting scenes of hills she had crossed, lanes she had followed, pubs she had passed and old ladies who had kindly refilled her water bottle. Her knowledge on the area south of Bristol, where I was for much of the week and where we enjoyed our weekends, certainly far exceeds mine.

In the New Year, Sandra and I started to build up stamina with a couple of LDWA cross-country runs around the Surrey hills. Getting out for a full day and covering 30 miles provides essential early season conditioning. These were followed by a 50Km race-walk around Burrator Reservoir, north of Plymouth, and then the 200Km Lagny race-walk in France.

Ideally we would have preferred at least one more ultra distance event. In 1988 I had built from one event to the next. The Land's End to John O'Groats run in September had been the culmination of a season which had seen me set a new record for running the length of Ireland (375 miles in 4½ days and a preparation for the British End-to-End), a new British 6 day running record on a road surface (517 miles set in New York on my way to 730 miles in a multi-day event), the successful defence of my National 100 mile race-walking title as well as various other events. Throughout the year I had covered nearly 3,500 miles in competition and 2,500 miles in training for a total of 5,936 miles.

To embark on a Land's End to John O'Groats so early in the

season was taking a risk. But the training over the winter and spring had been sustained and had gone well and at least my body was not over-tired from a long hard season.

Getting that balance right between building up the mileage and peaking for an event and not going over the top requires regular self assessment on weight, sleep patterns, eating, training times and general motivation. Over-training, getting ill (if not injured as well) has been the lot of too many top class British athletes, Seb Coe included. Careful and more scientific monitoring than we have generally been accustomed to in the UK is still needed.

Anybody aspiring to excellence has to have a rigorous, planned approach. The preparation has to be methodical and cover all the key aspects that will affect performance. Its implementation then has to be no less rigorously and closely monitored.

I stressed earlier the significance of targets. The detailed plan will be reflected in those targets. As they are met, we move along our path with increasing confidence and clarity towards the goal we have set. It is not by accident that excellence is achieved.

John and I now jogged gently along the road before we were interrupted by Claire Donnelly. She was arranging a live radio interview with BBC Radio Bristol. She ran alongside for a few moments holding her mobile phone before handing it over. I was on hold, listening to the preceding news item. Then it was my turn. *"So where are you now?"* *"Just passing Bristol Airport. I have missed the flight for Edinburgh so we're going to have to run there!"* There were the normal questions about how many miles a day and what are you eating and I made the standard phrase about being inspired by the Forrest Gump film to undertake this adventure. I managed to get in a plug for Sparks. We did the interview on the move at 6.30 am. Goodness knows who listens at that time on a Sunday morning. I believe they repeated it later.

Then it was off across the Cumberland Basin on the outskirts of Bristol. This was where Isambard Kingdom Brunel's SS Great Britain, the first steam powered screw propelled ship and the largest vessel in the world at the time had set sail for North America carrying passengers brought to Bristol on his Great Western Railway. Brunel had the vision of transporting people on his iron railroad to his iron steamship and thence across the Atlantic. A real package deal. It was not to last. The winding mud-silted River Avon was not suitable for large transatlantic liners and the trade passed to Cunard at Liverpool. The SS Great Britain ended as a hulk on the Falkland Islands until it was rescued and brought all the way back to Bristol on a floating barge where it now lies being refurbished in the same dry dock where it was built over 130 years ago.

A few hundred yards further up river, craftsmen were working on a replica of another famous ship. In 1497, John Cabot set off from the second city in the land, Bristol, in his boat the Matthew and discovered not just a few Caribbean Islands like Christopher Columbus, but new found land (Newfoundland) and the Canadian coast. The Matthew was now being recreated on the site where the original boat had been built, prior to it being sailed across the Atlantic to commemorate that epic voyage which had five hundred years earlier resulted in the discovery of the North American mainland.

We continued down the Avon Gorge and passed under the great memorial to Isambard Kingdom Brunel, his Avon Gorge, Clifton Suspension Bridge. The chains came from the old Hungerford Suspension Bridge in London when the chains intended for the Avon Gorge Bridge were used for his railway bridge over the Tamar between Devon and Cornwall.

After a couple more hours, we started to cross a bridge that seems to have stood the test of time less well than Brunel's Victorian edifices - the Severn Bridge. After major repairs, this road lifeline from and into Wales is being supplemented by a second Severn crossing. As we crossed the older version, the wind which has been hidden behind the hedges hits us, but not enough to take Don's breath away! After continuous nattering, I make my request; "Oh do please shut up just for a moment!" This caused slight surprise to James who thought I had been remarkably restrained so far. I also wondered if I should have blunted Don's enthusiasm especially when he bent right down to the ground. I then realised he had found a 2p coin. Dear old Don. He must be about the only person who has actually made a profit crossing the Severn Bridge!

As we stopped by Chepstow Racecourse for lunch, I wondered if he would do a circuit of the course - including the fences. He was utterly irrepressible.

130

Tintern Abbey must have one of the most glorious locations of any religious buildings in Britain. On a bend by the fast-flowing Wye and with steep wooded hills all around, it has an unexpected solemnity about it, no matter how many times it is revisited. As I caught a first glimpse of it through the sunlit trees on the long down hill run, I felt an inner glow. The cars passing me on the road were blotted out as my mind went out to embrace the tall dark stone nave and transept and take in the peaceful setting. I hardly noticed the coaches and tourists as we passed by and walked along the banks of the Wye.

The team also appreciated the serenity and splendour of the scene. The crew that was off-duty explored the site and enjoyed a couple of pints in the sunlight by the water. They said afterwards how they talked, joked and laughed and felt both united and truly motivated as a crew. It was well worth taking the scenic route north. Tintern Abbey certainly has the edge on Oldbury Nuclear Power Station. In a way it was a little reward and "pick you up" for all of us. Keeping the team motivated and enthused is as important as self motivation.

I had decided to leave the main Wye Valley road and go on the footpath across the fields. Derek bravely bumped along just behind over the molehills, manhandling his bike over styles and pushing it through tree-stumped woods. Maybe we lost a few minutes as a result, but it was so much better than being on the main road.

As we emerged from the footpath, Debbie met us with a bucket of iced water, a refreshing lolly and her normal encouragement. Then it was off across the stone bridge to continue on a disused railway line the other side of the river in the shelter of the trees, with the Wye gently flowing just a few yards away. We crossed the old railway bridge to rejoin the main road just south of Monmouth and put on a bit of a race-walking spurt as we passed a party of ramblers out for a Sunday afternoon stroll.

By the time Hugh Peers from SPARKS joined us, we were well on the way to Hereford. He was able to give us news on Sandra's progress. She had evidently passed our overnight stop less than an hour after we had left. This suggested that again she had had minimal sleep. Her tremendous commitment was obvious but I wondered how long she could keep going with such short snatches of sleep. Because she was still not able to run, she had subsequently fallen some 4 or 5 hours behind me. However, she seemed to be in good spirits and taking a steady realistic pace.

Hugh strode alongside in his white naval shorts while Angela leap-frogged us in the car until it was time for Hugh to leave us and join some friends for dinner in Hereford.

We had decided to encamp by Callow Church, overlooking that city, for our 7 pm sit down meal. It was a lovely position on the sunlit hills of what must have been the old road to Hereford. It was now bypassed and I could enjoy a few moments peace, while the van crews exchanged news on what they had been doing, how I had been going, changed over the main bag of gear and prepared for the next section.

Before the start of the event, Sandra and I had both set about organising a bag which would be transferred from one van to the other. On the Paris-Colmar race, this "black box" of essentials had contained the route description, the registration card that had to be stamped at each checkpoint, suntan lotion, anti-chafing cream, sun glasses and the main medical kit. Over time this bag of goodies had grown, so as to avoid us having duplicates of kit and waterproofs in each of the vans. It is always the way that, just after a change over of van crews, you decide that a particular vest is chafing under the arms and ask for a well-known over-sized replacement only to find that it has gone off with the other van and can't be retrieved. Shoes can also start to pinch and set up bad inflammation and blisters, whereas an early change of shoes which would ease the pressure on that particular spot can save a lot of pain later on.

We now, therefore, had a rather large bag which was transferred at every change-over point. It was also good discipline to ensure that all the clothes, shoes and other equipment that should be in it were kept together and passed over when they should be. It is all too easy for kit to be thrown into a van and lie there in a heap. If the clothes have been soaked in sweat or rain, you end up with a soggy heap. If the vans are kept tidy at all times then you have some chance of finding what you want at a moment's notice.

It all worked as planned; we almost began to suspect we were part of a highly professional organised outfit that really knew what it was doing!

Often I would ask Amos or Doug either for an article of

clothing or an item of food and seemingly just a few seconds later, there it would appear as though it was no problem. This quiet confidence gave me a great feeling that all was well and was going well. It may seem strange that such seemingly little things have such an effect. But when the mind does not have one hundred and one things to think about, it focuses on the little things. Get those right and it is happy. Get them wrong and the mind blows it up out of all proportion. I suppose it is rather like the person at home in a small community in New England or the Mid-West of the USA. Grand affairs of international politics and economics pass them by. What matters is the apparently petty, but nevertheless to them significant, tittle-tattle of local gossip and everyday happenings to which they can relate and over which they have some influence.

The same can be true in a company. It is fine for the directors to focus on the grand strategy, but what can drive productivity at the grass-roots can often be the apparently trivial. Remember the Hawthorne effect. Output went up when the level of lighting was increased. It then also went up again when it was decreased. What mattered was that somebody was paying some interest, some attention to what the workers were doing and hence the individuals felt they mattered.

Small rewards can have effects out of all proportion to their monetary value. Doug described to me how, as part of introducing the Baldridge Total Quality Approach, staff had been given a simple certificate to say they had suggested a given number of improvements which had then been implemented. The staff were delighted that their ideas and initiatives had been recognised and proudly displayed the certificates above their workplaces. This encouraged others to enter into the spirit of what almost became a game. *"Everyone started to enter into the spirit of putting forward ideas and seeing that they were not left out in having a certificate above their workplace. It was not so much a question of friendly rivalry but more of getting into a positive virtuous circle which produced personal thanks and recognition for the individual and cumulatively tremendous gains for the organisation. Motivating by example, by simple rewards and above all by recognition for an idea suggested or a job well done, is crucial to a team performance whatever the team."*

But how many managers really give it their full attention? They are so often focused upwards and externally on achieving their objectives or on "managing" downwards that they neglect the apparently trivial. It is however, these "trivial" drops of rain which can either build to a crescendo of annoyance and negative feedback (like rain on a corrugated iron roof) or can be channelled positively to create a flood of ideas which is unstoppable.

After our allotted dinner time stop by Callow Church, I thanked the crew that would now make its way to Leominster for the overnight stop. Doug had got a hotel room for me free of charge at the Tallot Hotel. I was definitely going to make Leominster by the time the bar and hotel closed! I set off at a good pace down the hill and enjoyed a sustained run in the evening sunshine to Hereford and out the other side. As the sun disappeared, we passed the SAS training ground behind its high and suitably impenetrable mixture of hedge and barbed wire. I wondered what the SAS would make of our adventure. Very character forming no doubt!

I remembered from the previous run that the hill before Leominster was rather similar to the Col du Bonhomme towards the end of the Paris-Colmar race. It had more than one false summit and many zig-zags through the woods. Just when you thought you were coming to the crest, it would go around another bend and continue rising. I made certain we ate and drank at the foot and continued to drink my Maxim carbohydrate supplement all the way to the top. Amos also remarked on its similarity to the French climb and was there at the top with a suitably large slice of malt loaf which I could chew on the long downhill run towards the distant cluster of lights which was to be our overnight stop.

After an hour or so, we entered the old border town of Leominster just after the pubs had closed and the locals were making their cheery way home or to the still open fish and chip shop. Some of them cheered us on our way, presumably having seen the sign on our van or maybe just from the effects of the beer. Any case I thought positively and waved back. I was surprised how much their support lifted me and how positively I joked in response after a fairly long hot day. Whether it was relief at achieving our objective on schedule or whether it was just the encouragement from strangers and new faces did not matter. Perhaps it was another example of the apparently trivial making a large impact and sending us to our beds contented and looking forward to the next instalment in our adventure.

The Talbot Inn in Leominster is a charming and old beamed coaching inn right in the town centre. We had kindly been offered a free room provided we used our own towels.

It was great to enjoy a good shower and stretch out on a real bed. James had set up the ultra-sound equipment, not so much because it was really needed but because it would provide additional deep massage for the calf muscles in particular that had had to work fairly hard up and down the various hills in Welsh border country.

We could also inspect the feet under the brighter bedroom lights and slap on appropriate amounts of Sudocrem antiseptic healing cream.

In the morning, we were out on the street by 5 am and Don and I set off through the old centre until Amos and breakfast caught us a couple of miles to the North.

Amos had decided to switch from Weetabix to muesli. This was good as it provided extra protein but had the disadvantage that, unless you soaked the muesli overnight, you ended up with a rather solid consistency sitting there in the breakfast bowl. Amos had rather overdone the amount of solids with the result that it just kept soaking up all the liquids put over it. When more liquid was added, the bowl began to overflow and I spent the next couple of miles leaving a trail of lumpy, milky muesli along the road with still more of it down my over-trousers. Eventually, I gave up and opted for a scrambled egg which Amos was getting a dab hand at producing, as he dashed from the driver's seat to his chef's position by the stove.

I had thought the route through Welsh border country to the south of Warrington would be particularly peaceful on a Bank Holiday Monday. I had not reckoned with the hundreds of motorbikes on their way to a meeting at Oulton Park. I'm afraid I was none too pleased as they kept speeding by in their great fart machines disturbing the peaceful scenery. When we approached one biker brushing down his fancy red leathers by the side of the road, while his bike steamed quietly to itself with its wheels in the air in a ditch, I was rather less than sympathetic. His mates however clustered around him like some tribe looking after an

135

injured warrior and a few moments later they all charged off in tribal pursuit, apparently none the worse for wear and presumably none the wiser.

For a few moments, all was peace and we could enjoy the dinosaur-like qualities of the hills around Church Stretton. The flanks of these hills seemed to narrow to a crest along the ridge just like a dinosaur's back with its elongated tail stretching away to the north.

It is remarkable how different the scenery is in different parts of England. You only have to travel a few miles for it to change. How different to North America, where you can travel over a thousand miles and not really notice any difference in the landscape. I wonder if I was put down blindfolded by helicopter in different counties and then the blindfold was removed, whether I could identify where I was. I suspect I would have a pretty good hit rate.

As the evening drew in, the wind began to freshen from the north and we all put on another layer of clothing. Doug had arranged overnight accommodation at a campsite just a hundred yards off the A49 south of Warrington, and we were able to reach this by midnight with another 80 miles under our belt.

When you look at the map, it seems a long way from Chepstow to Warrington. But we had covered the distance from lunchtime on Sunday to close of play on Monday - across Wales in one and a half days.

I thanked the crews for their great efforts during the day. We had enjoyed some marvellous scenery, overcome the Oulton bikers and were some miles ahead of where we had been last time I had done the run. I wanted them to know that we were doing well.

The following are some general thoughts:

Excellence is not achieved by accident. A lot of hard training based on detailed schedules and close monitoring underlay the physical preparation.

In an event "dissociation" can be a positive mental approach. Drawing inspiration from what is around you can provide both mental relaxation and stimulation. It may even be worth a detour from the straight milestone marked path. The achievement of the objective will not be compromised and the individual and team may come back reinvigorated as a result. The "detour" can be physical, as in our case, or an evening or day out from work in different surroundings. This can be a way of saying "thank you" for all the often unsaid little things on which success is built.

Rewarding and motivating a team is too often neglected in the pursuit of cold rational quantified objectives. The hard edges of corporate life need to be softened. Attention to the apparently trivial can yield high returns.

None of us are automatons driven solely by financial rewards. We all need someone to say "well done" and "thank you" for a job well done.

12

On to Edinburgh

The A49 around Warrington is a horrible road. Full of heavy lorries of all shapes and sizes, it funnels traffic at you from all directions at round-a-bouts, traffic lights and unexpected junctions.

While the Manchester ship canal and Mersey crossing have their fleeting moments of interest, there is little else to commend this part of industrial Lancashire. I just gritted my teeth and bore it as best I could until we were in more open country and could look over to Winter Hill and know we were in more friendly territory south of Preston.

I had worked for 2 years at the truck and bus plant at Leyland and had stayed at Chorley. Sandra had come up most weekends on the train and, after dinner in a couple of favourite dives in Preston, we would enjoy walks around the local hills, or speeding early in the morning up the motorway to the Lake district, over westwards to the sea (including the lights of Blackpool) or eastwards to the Pennines. It had been a marvellous 2 years and we had made many friends in the area.

As we approached Preston, one of those friends kindly came to meet us.

John Wilson ("Doctor John") had been in Product Planning at Leyland's truck and bus until he left to become a lecturer at the polytechnic, now the university in Preston. He conducted the Leyland Male Voice Choir, in which I had sung, and was a methodist lay preacher. He and his wife Janet became godparents to our daughter Victoria, in addition to being godparents to a least half a dozen cats that roamed freely around their bungalow. Each had a dramatic story to tell of being abandoned somewhere but eventually finding a home with this friendly couple. Victoria is in her element every time she visits them and follows the chequered life history of the cat family with great interest.

John is an active hill walker but also loves his food. And it shows! His friendly, bear-like form now strode towards us on an old railway track we had decided to take. This took us across the River Ribble and right into the heart of Preston, well away from the traffic. Doug was cycling with me with a tucker bag of goodies to keep me going, while the van followed the normal route and would meet us on the A6 going north.

John expertly navigated us through the back streets of Preston, fearlessly striding in front of the traffic at round-a-bouts as we ran across. After a mile or so and slightly out of breath, he retreated to his students and left us to our own devices.

The crew now told me that Sandra was having some real problems with her feet and had asked for help from James. Claire Donnelly from Countrywide had been despatched in her car to rendezvous with us and take James back. This was of course fine by me, as he was clearly needed much more with Sandra.

It was then that we realised why Claire stuck limpet-like close to our vans and then to Sandra's. She had been issued with a map about the size you get in a pocket diary. Not surprisingly, for most of the journey so far, she had no real idea exactly where she was and certainly no capability of finding her own way if she had become detached from us. It was all she could do to travel on the M6 and meet up with James' van at a motorway junction, north of Preston.

Cyril promptly went out and bought her a decent map and from then on there was no holding her!

My own crew guided me expertly through Lancaster using shopping precincts and one-way streets and so over the bridge towards our planned dinner stop.

However, with the underside of my left foot becoming increasingly painful, I felt I needed to rest before the scheduled stop. We therefore called up the other van and pulled into a side street on the outskirts of Lancaster. Immediately we were surrounded by a pack of animated children wanting to know everything from the route we were taking, to what we were eating and drinking, to what my feet looked like and why I was now strapping large plasters over them. Cyril spun them all sorts of yarns but we did not turn them away.

I felt like Louis XIV ("The Sun King") who would open the

doors of his bedchamber and allow the masses to come in and watch him sitting in bed eating his boiled egg and the rest of his breakfast. The eager faces of our spectators were hungry for information on anything and everything and I wondered if one of them would eventually take up this mad ultra-distance sport. I hoped not for their sake!

After forty minutes I backed myself carefully out of the van and gingerly started to walk towards the Lake District. Fortunately, our baggage train was persuaded to stay behind and soon it was the old partnership of Doug and myself striding up the road together.

We had left Debbie at Preston Station, as she had used up the leave she could spare. Somehow she had not managed to say a proper goodbye at the lunchtime change over point and that had strangely upset and disappointed me. She had been a great help and inspiration and good team member (and it's not easy for a girl to mix in with all the blokes) and I had wanted to say "thank you" before she departed. I expressed my disappointment to Doug and, sure enough the next day, Debbie phoned to ask on our progress and specifically to speak to me. The feeling that might otherwise have gnawed into me was thereby satisfied. I mused again on how fairly inconsequential things can prey on the mind.

Just as dusk was settling, a great cross-country fell runner and London to Brighton stalwart, David Rosen, passed us in his car, waved and said he would park 5 miles up the road and jog back. Soon his springing style was coming down the road towards us and I responded with a good spell of jogging and nattering into the darkness, as the miles slipped past.

Reinvigorated by fresh company and an increased pace, and with Doug telling me about some of the places we were passing which he knew so well, we met the Kendal Bypass and jogged on towards our overnight campsite on the outskirts of the town as it lay cradled in the foothills of the Lake District.

Amos locked the doors of his van to get a good night's sleep. Five minutes later, James and Ian walked straight in! After they had gone, Amos re-locked it and at 5 am next morning I walked straight in as he had overslept!

As I started off slightly annoyed, I looked back to see the ever zealous Don running up the hill behind me with my carbohydrate drink. I also experienced the strange sight of Cyril running across

140

the open camp field from Amos's van to Doug's in his underpants. He looked like some lover that had been caught *in flagrante delicto* by the returning husband! Any slight annoyance evaporated as I laughed and strode off with Don scampering behind me.

We had thought to rendezvous with Boyd's wife, Lillian (an international race-walker in her own right) who lived nearby. However, I thought it would be a bit unsocial to phone her at 5 am, so we walked through the quiet, deserted lanes of Kendal by ourselves trying to eat Amos's muesli.

This time he had not put so much in the bowl so at least it did not leave a trail for all the dogs and cats of Kendal to follow. It was still, however, too solid as he had forgotten to soak it overnight. Amidst much coughing and spluttering as wheatflakes got caught in my throat, I slowly reduced the bulk in the bowl before tipping the remainder quietly behind a bush out of sight of the van.

I took an extra marmalade sandwich as we approached the long climb up and over Shap. At over 2,000 ft, this would be the longest haul of the journey so far only to be exceeded by the 2 passes either side of Aviemore in Scotland.

The climb is steady with the occasional flat section on which a farmhouse perches, looking out over the valley. Lambs were venturing forth from their mums and pretending to eat the grass, while large well fattened cattle lumbered around the steep hillsides.

The valley road below us petered out into a track by an old stone bridge. No doubt when the snows were melting, the stream would be white with activity, but now it was just a trickle from which a few lazy cows were having their breakfast drink. A farm with its dark granite walls and outhouses nestled beneath the steep crags at the end of the track. I wondered how many generations had lived there and how often they were cut off in the winter. I thought of Postman Pat trudging through the snow to deliver the letter or parcel of Mail Order clothes and of the now silent chimney alive with light and smoke in the winter months.

The tree line which had clothed the electricity pylons, gave way to open barren rock and heather and revealed the line of steel structures standing stark against the sky-line ahead. The skeletons were out of sympathy with the rolling crags and subtle changes of earthen colours. The lowing of the wind in the wires with which they held hands suggested they wished they were not there either in their exposed positions but tucked neatly underground.

Derek had bravely decided to cycle up Shap. He was now in a very low gear on his mountain bike and breathing at least as hard as I was. The head wind we had faced since the start was still there, and as we crested the final rise it fairly whistled past us. It was 7 am and I suggested to Derek that as the shops were just opening, he might like to free-wheel back down to Kendal, buy a morning paper and they cycle back up again for the exercise and to keep warm. He didn't take to this idea but rather put on another layer of clothing for the long exposed descent.

The scenery changes over the ridge. The views are spoilt by an unsightly quarry gashed out of the mountainside. The noise of machines disturbs the early morning, as they cart away the granite to unsightly neighbouring works covered in dust and belching white smoke. Equally deforestation adds to the desolate scene, as dead stumps of conifers recently hacked down poke through the tangled undergrowth. No wonder the whole area is outside the National Park boundaries.

After a few miles, the vans swapped over and James appeared on the bike. A couple more miles and Amos's van passed us, with Don jumping up and down inside like some caged monkey. He was let out and came scampering up the road. Evidently James still had the ignition keys to the other van in his pocket! Don grabbed them and like a friendly hyena danced back to Amos who phoned through with the good news.

The reception was not that great and Amos had difficulty being understood. Don's repeated interruptions and technical advice on how to operate a mobile phone soon led to a loud "shut up!" from Amos, and Don being despatched to do penance with me for a few minutes, while Amos drove back to Doug.

Poor Don. He talked away partly to me and partly to himself vowing that he would stop arguing with Amos and accept what he was told. The dynamics of Amos's van were interesting to say the least. But so long as Amos's word was accepted as law and his leadership obeyed, it all seemed to work. At least everyone knew their place!

Carlisle hides in the valley behind the tree-lined hills with just its spires and chimneys visible at first. The outskirts sprawl a bit, but the stone clad centre around the towered castle and wide main shopping streets have a granite solidity. We nipped across a flower-lined park and down an underpass with interesting three dimensional murals which seemed cunningly to have defeated or deflected the normal graffiti vandal. My calf muscles however rebelled at having to go down and up steps and it was with some relief that the two vans were parked nose to tail near a fine stone bridge which spanned the wide river. I sat down gratefully on the tailboard of one of the vans and James massaged my calves.

We had tried to get through to Boyd and his crew on the mobile phones, as we wanted to find the telephone number of Nigel Robinson. As the leader of our previous expedition, and as someone who lived not far away by the Roman Wall, I knew he intended to come out and support. But either Boyd had switched off the phone or they were ascending the far side of Shap and were out of contact. If the latter was the case, that would make them about 10 hours behind us. I doubted Sandra had slowed so much and got increasingly and unnecessarily agitated as to what was happening and why we could not contact anyone.

The head wind also began to affect me, as it blew across the open countryside around the Solway Firth. For the first time since Lands End, I began to feel a bit tired and thought that the elements were deliberately conspiring against me. I was beginning to fall a prey to negative thoughts and had to snap out of it.

I focused on the roadside signs which had the Cross of St Andrew against the second village down. I guessed that must mean the Scottish Border. It did not matter what the village was called. It was that St Andrew's sign which interested me.

I also remembered that last time we had just got over the Scottish Border before stopping for the night. This time we should be over 4 hours up on that. In other words, we would be over 1 hour inside Don Ritchie's record. I repeated that reassuring thought and shouted in my mind what I could remember from a speech by King Lear:
"Blow wind and crack your cheeks,
You cataracts and hurricanes blow
Till you have cracked the steeples, drowned the cocks."
I turned my annoyance into a positive force and pumped my arms as I raised my walking pace. "I will beat you, you bloody

wind; you will not beat me. I will get this record despite you. Nothing you can throw at me will stop me."

I got Derek to cycle just ahead of me so I was right on his rear wheel. "This will offer some protection from the wind" I called. "Try and keep it steady."

We battled on for over an hour until I realised that I was not getting much wind protection and my frustration returned. I called to Amos to put his van in front to provide a more effective shield.

Amos had the van with the rear door so he could fix it open and look in his rear view mirror to see where I was. He now tried to keep just a couple of yards ahead. It was tiring work for him with the foot hardly on the accelerator. I jogged behind the van and Don helped Amos by shouting the occasional "slower" or "up a bit." They worked well as a team, and I smiled as Amos asked Don "OK? How are we doing?" Don felt needed. Together we would all make it. I knew that even more now.

As we crossed the Scottish Border we all gave a cheer. Derek took a picture.

It was a good wide road and fortunately there was not much traffic. The other van passed us with great wavings and toots and I looked at my watch. It would soon be dinner time. "Great. One last effort and then I can relax for a bit."

I had also promised to phone my nine year old daughter, Victoria, before we hit too many hills and mountains which would affect the reception. I had only spoken to her once so far, though I knew Sandra had phoned a couple of times.

It was wonderful to speak to her, to tell her we were now in Scotland and she could look on the map and see where we were. She sounded in excellent spirits. She had just had her sports day and had run 6½ miles non stop. She was so proud. For her it was the equivalent of our End-to-End. It was her way of associating herself with what we were doing, of being part of our race, part of a great family adventure in which everyone gave of their best. I pictured her lovely smiling face in my mind and her natural exuberance and enthusiasm. The word "daddy" and her blowing me kisses down the phone brought a dryness to my mouth and I brushed away a couple of tears.

I looked at the lovely rolling hills around the Eden Valley. How well named. The wind had relented and it was peaceful with lengthening shadows and the noise of evening bird-song. I felt I could walk in these hills forever and never tire.

After refuelling with dinner and having the normal massage from James, I set off into the sunset in a state of calm contentment, so different from the mood of battling frustration just a couple of hours earlier.

I marched up the road, humming away to myself and taking in the glorious scenery. As I turned a corner, there standing by the roadside was Nigel Robinson. "I thought you might be on this stretch. We've just driven back from Surgeres. Yiannis Kouros set a new World 48 hour record. But boy it was hot."

We nattered away like long lost brothers, as I raised my walk into a jog. The van crews handed Nigel a water bottle and left us to it. They were no doubt as pleased as me to see him, after I had been pestering them for so many hours asking them to get in contact and tell Nigel where we were.

"Hey, you're going great. Everything OK?"

"Yes" I responded, "I'm going well. We're well up on last time and inside the record. I just have to keep it going."

It was marvellous to see him. It gave me such a boost.

Nigel had literally just dumped Eleanor and son, Myles, at their home and sped off to join us. After a few miles he returned to his car and undertook to find and support Sandra next morning.

My crew rejoined me and we pushed on up the winding hill into the darkness. I wanted to make it over the ridge before we stopped. Amos went ahead to spy out a suitable overnight spot and Doug drove with his lights illuminating the route ahead. At around midnight, when we had successfully achieved our objective and were over the pass, we pulled into a quarry right by the roadside and sank thankfully to sleep.

The morning saw us through Hawick with its woollen mills by the river, and a couple of early morning runners who wished us well. Then it was over the hills through Selkirk with its even larger mill complex where the fine Selkirk glass is made and over more hills to Galashiels.

Doug guided me with his town map on the shortest route. His van stopped by a roadside cafe advertising home made cakes. When they had bought a suitably tempting selection and explained what we were doing, the old lady that owned the shop donated a hot jacket potato with a mixed bean sauce for my lunch. It was very kind and provided some excellent fuel for the afternoon. I thought how friendly people can be and how apparently trivial events can produce a morale raising response - when you want them to!

Amos had meanwhile parked in a side street for their lunch. A local resident was washing his car but had evidently forgotten to close a window! He didn't seem to care too much that the inside of his car was rather wet and, while he was waiting for it to dry out, kindly hosed down Amos's van. Amos made certain all his windows were closed!

The local police were less friendly. As an ex policeman, Amos seems to attract them. He had been flagged down on the A30 in Devon when driving behind me. And he was now flagged down and told that his Road Tax disc had fallen off!

Later on he parked in a farm entrance at dusk, as Derek and I came past. The farmer rushed up to find out if he and Cyril were trying to break into his farmhouse, as apparently someone had tried to do a few days before. Cyril not only reassured him, but also got him as a witness for the Guinness Book of Records. Never missing an opportunity and never a dull moment!

As we skirted Edinburgh, making for the Forth Road Bridge, we were joined by John Taylor from the Hundred Kilometre Association. This long distance running club was founded some years ago by Ron Hindley and his wife, great enthusiasts from Sandra's home town of Grantham.

John had driven many miles to park his car on the north side of the Forth Road Bridge and then run south to meet us. Nearing the end of the day, I was not capable of running the long uphill slope which led towards the bridge, so we walked together on the grass verge, as traffic rattled past us and my crew bravely dared the juggernauts to get me drink and food from the other side of the dual carriageway.

Eventually we made it to the suspension bridge with its surprisingly high hump in the centre, up which we walked before jogging down the other side. To the right was the great Victorian iron structure of the Forth Road Bridge illuminated by thousands and thousands of light bulbs courtesy of Scottish Power. Its giant lozenge shapes and great girders seem to epitomise the strength and sure foundation of a Victorian era. I remembered the sequence in

146

the film The Thirty Nine Steps and the numerous pictures of steam trains and the record breaking Mallard. I was sorry to hear that it was falling into the state of sad repair with rusty bits even falling of it. Gone are the days when that famous aphorism was true about starting repainting at one end of the Forth Bridge as soon as you had finished painting at the other end.

It was just beginning to rain as we went up the hill just before Kelty. We had done over 76 miles and with the rain starting to come on heavy, it seemed as good a place as any to bed down for the night. We had covered over 570 miles in a week and were over two thirds of the way to our destination. I hoped the rain would signify a change in the direction of the wind and I went to sleep praying for a good south westerly to help us over the next three days.

Problems and obstacles can be a source of negative annoyance and worry or they can be challenges to be faced and overcome. The positive mind will opt for the latter. Just give it a space to think laterally.

Equally, apparently trivial signs of encouragement and support, or a break in what could just become a routine, can raise morale and motivation. Team players need to appreciate the significance of the apparently inconsequential. Few can be fuelled forever just on a vision. We also need regular injections of more mundane stimuli to get us through the long patches of the everyday and ordinary.

13

Crisis in the Snow

By 5 am the rain had stopped and the wind was again in the north west. I cursed to Derek as we set off with him holding the bowl of muesli and me slurping mouthfuls. At least Amos had now got round to soaking the muesli overnight and getting a good consistency. The wretched wind however was a mental pain, even though it was only light. Probability theory suggested that it really was about time we had some favourable winds!

The light breeze was blowing the clouds away and a soft dawn was rising beyond the low hills out to sea. I thought of the rain in the night and what a long downpour would do to the dressings on my poor feet. I decided that perhaps I was not quite so hard done by after all. In any case, there was nothing we could do about the weather.

A long gentle downhill slope got me into running gear and the disappointment about the wind was soon put to the back of my mind. The villages were also different to those we had encountered south of Edinburgh. The older houses were made of a gaunt block stone often painted white. Sometimes they were just single storey like crofters' cottages. Elsewhere dormer windows had been punched through the roof or mock crenellations added to the corners. The occasional French chateau style town hall or bank rose in town centres to look down on its lowly brethren, while groups of standard local authority dwellings could be seen in small estates down back streets. Milk floats and children delivering papers were the only signs of life. The M90 seemed to have taken most of the traffic, leaving us to enjoy the old route.

As we turned into a Glen, the sheer joy of the enclosed scenery won me over. The sun shone through the fresh new green leaves while the river bubbled beside us. The birds sang all around us and the spring flowers, which we had enjoyed weeks earlier in the south of England but which had now finished there, were here in all their brightness. It was like going back in time. I re-experienced the daffodils and crocuses, the celandines and the first bluebells all mixed in together. I seemed especially favoured, as though our little team had been singled out to have a repeat performance of early spring.

There was hardly a car on the road as I ran with Derek in a relaxed style in and out of the sun and shade and patterns of trees. I thought how lucky we were to be out here in the open experiencing something that few others have the opportunity to experience or even contemplate. This was what it was all about. *"Let's fix this experience, this peace and pleasure firmly in our minds and draw on it in the future,"* I said to myself. I felt we could run down this valley forever.

Eventually we reached the flood plain and the vans changed shifts. Cyril asked a garage attendant if I could please use their toilet and he obliged, ushering me into the back where I could also splash water on my face. The owner wished us well and the old lady receptionist stared somewhat bemused from her glass cell, as we trotted off down the road.

Perth lies hidden over a low range of hills when you approach it from the south. The motorway is above you and you see the exit signs for this "Gateway to the Highlands," but it is only when you climb over the shoulder of the hill that it reveals itself in the next valley.

I remembered that last time we had eaten our dinner overlooking the city. Suddenly I had jumped up, clambered out of the van and started running down the hill, across some playing fields and through the city centre. I had mentally miscalculated and had convinced myself that we would not break the record unless I did a hundred miles that day. My medical support diagnosed an imbalance of salts and, after they had caught me, handed over a bottle of Ribena drink which was strong enough to disguise the salt they had added. After I slowed, they quietly took me through the calculations which of course showed that I was well within the record time. Only then did I relax.

There was no mad dash this time. Doug, Cyril and I walked across the playing fields which cut off two sides of the triangle, and then strode through the city with its broad and graceful streets, and onto the dual carriageway beyond. A lorry driver asked us the way to an industrial estate. Doug duly gave him appropriate directions from his town map as though he were a local. Since Doug was dressed in a violently coloured Costa del Concrete tee shirt, this seemed highly unlikely, and I wondered why the driver had picked on us.

I reckoned we were now seven hours up on last time and hence four hours inside the record. I told the others and we all celebrated with a cup of coffee and some chocolate biscuits..

The A9 would be our home for virtually the next three days. North of Perth, it is a bit like the A30 in Devon and Cornwall in that it is often dual carriageway and with fairly gentle rises and descents. The scenery, however, becomes more and more dramatic as you approach the Grampian Mountains. Pine forests clothe the lower reaches of hills and the broad River Tay moved majestically and invitingly in the shimmering heat.

I suggested to my crew that they take the detour by the old road to visit Dunkeld with its charming little houses and town square. They preferred to stay in close support but said they appreciated the offer.

It was a wonderful afternoon and we all had the great feeling that we were in the Highlands, seeing them in their spring freshness and friendliness and making really good progress. The French baronial style Pitlochry Hotel lay across our path and we left the main road to go by its side, past Blair Atholl Distillery with its rows of stone sheds - no doubt housing a few million pounds worth of the hard stuff - and past an old chap stretched out on a park bench who looked as though he had had his fill from one of the barrels.

Little did we know that Sandra was to experience her major crisis a day or so later around this town. She had been trying to get by on minimal sleep for over seven days. With extremely deep blistered heels, with lapses of navigational efficiency and awareness from her crew and hence overall with more mental pressure, she had virtually collapsed in Pitlochry. Lucy had sought support from a lady who turned out to be intensely caring and Sandra had taken a relaxing bath in her house and then slept for 8 hours. Her second van however was not made aware of what was happening and spent an anxious time going up and down the dual carriageway trying to find her. When eventually contact was made, everyone was fairly frazzled and only about 20 miles was negotiated in that fraught 24 hour period.

I was fortunately in better shape. My feet were certainly blistered with the centre underside of my left foot particularly painful. Every time I started after a rest period, I had to try and blot out the pain until it could become numbed and I could forget about it. It was a good reason for keeping rest periods to a minimum! I also found myself nodding off in the early afternoon while walking along the road. Whether this was my natural circadian rhythm, the effects of lunch or of the hottest part of the day, I don't know. I had, however, continually to refocus on the objectives and make certain I kept eating and drinking to maintain my energy stores.

Our dinner stop was on the old road at Killiecrankie. This conjured up a couple of associations. First of course there is the marvellous site itself owned by the National Trust for Scotland. The deep gorge with the river bubbling below and a narrow tree-lined path on the steep hillside shows how obvious an ambush point this was for the Highlanders who descended on the column of King George's men. But it also reminded me of Mr Killiecrankie in Raoul Dahl's book George's Marvellous Medicine. *"He was a kind father to George, but inclined to get over excited at the smallest things. The enormous chicken in the yard was no small thing. 'It's enormous, it's gigantic, it's tremendous' ..... etc"*

It's a marvellous thing reading children's books. So many of them are often wasted on children!

We had in fact made such good progress that the other van was slightly late catching us. This led to more than a mild expression of annoyance on my part. I had mentally psyched myself to get to Killiecrankie at 7pm for dinner. I said to Amos that was to be our objective. Here we now were on time. I felt I had done really well and fulfilled my part of the bargain. I was also pretty worn out and wanted my rest and reward. Surely all the crew had to do was sit in their van, drive to the dinner stop and get the food. Why couldn't they just do that simple thing? How could they possibly be late?

"Where have you been?" I snapped, when their cheery faces passed me in their van. It was not a very kind welcome for a crew

151

just coming on duty full of enthusiasm. To them my reaction was, I am sure, both unfeeling and unreasonable.

After nearly eight days, the mind was beginning to show the strain. It would last out for the time it had set itself, keep the body moving forward, keep the pain under control, keep itself motivated. But if it reached that time critical point and the expected reward was not there, it did not have the reserves to keep going - at least not without some release of tension.

I also felt hungry, and I always get a bit annoyed when I'm hungry.

I collapsed into the van. James said how incredible it was that I had moved so far in the afternoon. That gave me a boost and I repeated to myself that yes we had done well. I started to relax and apologised for snapping at them a few moments earlier.

I remembered how it had been to support others on ultra distance events. I have helped Sandra and Nigel Robinson in 24 hour races and manned check points on LDWA events. You want to be associated with the runners. You want to share their experiences. Of course you cannot because they are doing the event and you are outside looking in. But you want to feel your support is important and you are part of the race even though you cannot experience the feelings of the athlete. You cannot feel them yourself.

Hence you hang on their every word, their every expression. Any signal as to their state gives you an insight into their feelings and draws you closer in to the event.

So it was with my crews. They would come back on duty and immediately want to know everything I had said. Every snippet was eagerly devoured and dissected. Every compliment and positive remark made them feel ten feet tall and inspired them to still greater efforts.

How careless, how thoughtless, how destructive of me to respond in a negative way to anything. I tried to be smiling and positive whenever I could. But I also had to focus on the task when I was on the road. The breaks were the best times to show my thanks. And they passed all too quickly.

It was a great tribute to my crews that they let the intemperate remark pass without a response or a subsequent reference. Perhaps they knew and understood. Maybe we were more united and more

152

jointly committed to our single objective than I appreciated. In the grand scheme of things, the odd remark could be put aside, eventually to be recalled in fun and thereby transformed.

Ian introduced a great slice of pizza. Bliss! Heaven! I had wondered whether we might enjoy a pizza dinner and had mentioned the possibility earlier, but had not dared to hope that one might be found. But here it was, all deep baked and golden, and there was another slice if I wanted it. I lay back and relaxed even more. What a difference a pleasant surprise and reward can make - even a simple slice of pizza!

I laughed and joked and looked at the wonderful steep valley with its fresh green trees shining bright in the sunlight. There was nowhere else in the world I wanted to be. If only Sandra was also here to share the delight of this glorious spring day.

"Give to me the life I love.
Let the way go 'fore me ...
All I ask, the heaven above
And the road before me. "

I devoured a remarkable three slices while James massaged my legs back into action. I backed myself down out of the van and away I went into the setting sun with the newborn lambs bleating on either side and jumping and skipping in the fields. I was fully revived, even if not quite up to jumping around with the lambs. The mountains were now all around and I could see the main road snaking its way in a great sweep towards the setting sun before it did its unseen turn to the north and the long run down to Aviemore. Blair Atholl stood out white amongst the trees in the hillside over to our right and an ominous bank of clouds built up over the mountains behind. As night fell, we could feel the temperature drop as we continued to climb. Down below to our left, a diesel rail car trundled up the line. No doubt its steam engine predecessors would have laboured up this long incline.

We put on another layer of clothing as the wind became even colder. What looked like mist up ahead became a flurry of sleet and soon we were catching the edge of it. We pulled our hoods even further over our peaked caps and Doug and Cyril moved just in front to try and provide a bit of protection and to help keep the pace going. I wanted to make it over Drumochter Pass before we stopped.

On 3 or 4 occasions we had approached a hill around the time for our night stop. On each occasion, I had insisted we get over the crest. The hills became milestones which had to be passed before I could take my reward.

At around midnight, the road started to drop, but I was still not convinced we had reached the summit and fully rounded the corner. However, with laybys not very frequent, and with everyone getting increasingly cold in the wind and recurring flurries of sleet, we retreated into the next layby and spent a night disturbed by the wind and the shaking of the vans, as overnight juggernauts thundered by just a few feet from us.

In the morning at 5 o'clock it was a struggle to crank myself out of the van and start the slow process of moving off down the road. But down it was, and I was pleased that we had definitely gone over the pass.

Amos's muesli had been warmed with hot milk which made a good rich porridge. But in the cold, the benefit was soon lost. With double pairs of gloves and two layers of trousers over my tracksuit bottoms, I still could not get properly warm.

The early morning sun was striking the snow clad tops of the mountain ranges and the grand and vast scenery all around should have inspired me to take advantage of a good downhill slope and run all the way to the valley. But somehow I just could not get myself moving. I could not loosen up enough to break into a run and felt I was wasting the long downhill. I remembered how I had run all this section last time in the afternoon. But while I knew I was up on last time I was worried that I couldn't run. Would I now slip behind the clock? Why couldn't I run? "Come on, force yourself!" I tried a few paces but just could not keep it going. My thighs seemed very stiff and tired. Maybe they were still cold. Perhaps things would feel better when the sun had warmed everything a bit more.

I strode out as best I could. We passed the distillery at Dalwhinney over to our left "the highest in Scotland" and kept to the main road past Kingussie to join the old road to Kincraig.

I nipped behind some bushes; and when I emerged, there 100 yards ahead was Don Ritchie and his wife Isabel talking to my crew. The current Lands End to John O'Groats record holder had driven over from Speyside to see how I was doing. Because he had

154

a fractured bone in one foot and was resting it, he took his bike from the back of his estate car and cycled alongside. We compared notes on our previous record-breaking runs and I confirmed I was on schedule to set a new record.

Anyone going for records or for victory in any event, has to play to their strength. In a long track race, the person with the fast finish will try and slow a race so the kick finish can be used to best effect. Someone without that fast finish may have to settle for leading from the front and hoping to burn off the competition on the way. Don's strength is his ability to run marathon distances and above at a fast pace. His 100 km times are incredible, especially for someone who has just passed 50 years of age. In 1989 he had therefore run 3 hard marathons everyday interspersed with 3 hour rest periods, during which he would relax, refuel and revive himself. His approach was thus completely different from mine which relies on keeping going, for the most part eating and drinking on the move and playing to my own strength of fast walking interspersed with periods of jogging (I am reluctant to call it running) especially on the downhill slopes.

Partly I suspect for the sake of appearances now that Don had joined us, and maybe because the road was flat and hence imposed less of a strain on the thighs, I forced myself into a brief jog, which Isabel filmed. My right knee however was hurting and I saw little point in aggravating it further. I suggested to Doug that we try and find a campsite for lunch where James could fix up the ultrasound machine and we could have a go at the muscles just above the knee which seemed to be the particular problem.

Doug looked on his map and camp guide and fortunately there was a campsite just a couple of miles up the road before Aviemore. We pulled in just as a dark cloud unleashed its sleet on us and James got to work while I enjoyed some rice, vegetables and chicken.

James turned the ultrasound up fairly high to get the maximum effect. I felt as though I was having nervous convulsions. The sleet passed and we drove back the 200 yards to the campsite entrance, where I gingerly lowered myself back onto the road and began walking. The knee if anything was stiffer than before and there was no question of my attempting to run on it. I hoped that it might loosen. With Don cycling by my side and Isabel continuing to take the odd video clipping, I certainly was not going to let on the potential seriousness of the problem. In any case, we had a long climb ahead of us and I had no intention of running up Slocht, which was to be the highest pass on the End-to-End.

As we set off up the long climb, the clouds closed in and the occasional flurry of sleet hitting our light waterproofs turned into something much more serious. The cars coming towards us had their headlights on and windscreen wipers still working. We knew we were in for a hard time ahead.

The wind was now blowing fiercely in our faces and sleet was hitting us with considerable force. As soon as I could, I changed out of my lightweight waterproofs into the heavier version, and first Don and then Derek went ahead to try and provide a bit of protection from what was increasingly turning into a blizzard. Don was getting blown about on his bike and covered in sleet and snow with just his face peering out from under a large woolly hat. Derek and I marched step for step as the slush and water began to stream down the road and the cars and lorries sprayed us with more as they passed close by.

I kept as close behind Derek as possible and Amos never let us out of his sight. He would pull the van into a layby ahead and rush out with food and a warm drink of chocolate Slim Fast. It may seem strange to be knocking back a slimming drink on such an event and in such conditions, but they actually contain a very good balance of minerals, vitamins, protein and essential nutrients. Provided they do not fill you up too much and you can keep on eating and drinking, they provide a useful supplement to the more regular Maxim which was my staple carbohydrate drink.

I imagined I was slipstreaming behind Derek and focused my mind on the back of his waterproof jacket. Driving my arms and willing myself to do battle with the elements, we fought on, even when Don gave up the fight and retreated back home in his estate car. I thanked him for his support and the spirit of comradeship which had led him to turn out (though I knew he was also spying on how I was tackling the event so he could learn a few tricks for any future assault of his own).

Over the top, the wind seemed to drop and the sleet turned to snow. We took the side road through Moy and, on the flat, I attempted a few yards of jogging. I soon limped to a halt, as the

156

pain was just too great. I was now limping even while walking and inevitably slowing as a result. My feet were sodden from the slush and I knew the dressings and the blistered skin underneath would be a dreadful mess. As the snow continued to fall and I got slower and colder, all I could think of was just getting to the vans that were parked a mile or so ahead. We had called them both together for an early evening dinner, as I did not think I could last out till 7 o'clock. They lay by the snow covered banks, shielded partly from the wind by some pine trees but still looking lonely, cold and wet.

As I approached them, I could not bear to look at Amos as I knew he would see the tears rolling down my cheeks. I therefore turned my back behind the van and pretended to nip to the loo. I had given everything into the sleet and wind and was now exhausted both mentally and physically. My injured knee and inability even to walk properly drained my mind of all positive emotion. I felt like an empty tin can standing there exposed, shivering and drained in the snow.

James helped me up into the van and I collapsed on the cushions that made up our bed.

I was all in. With my wet gloves still on I felt my right thigh through my waterproof over trousers. It was incredibly swollen. I could hardly get the waterproofs off. Neither could I bend the right knee. James helped me. I was shocked to see that the knee and lower thigh had swollen to a size about 50% more than normal. The shock woke me out of my tiredness. It also obviously alarmed James and the rest of the crew.

James tested the knee by pressing down on it and getting me to pull and push it against his resistance. There did not appear to be any torn ligaments. I contorted myself into other positions, as he prodded and probed. Each movement, though difficult, did not produce serious pain. That was reassuring.

James had been speaking to his mentor Jonathan in Bristol. They had discussed the possible diagnosis. James was now able to confirm what they had suspected.

"The patella has come partly out of its groove. Normally you race and train facing the traffic with the camber falling away to the right. We have just done about seven hundred miles on the left hand side of the road and so with the camber sloping to the left.

The knee has rebelled. It can't take any more of that."

There was silence. I suppose I was slightly relieved. At least we knew what was wrong. I placed myself entirely in James's hands.

"What shall we do?" I asked in a subdued voice.

"I can strap it firmly and tightly to stop the patella moving further and ideally try and get it back where it should be. It will be uncomfortable and there is some risk of chafing, but there's not much else we can do. In normal circumstances I would tell you to rest it, but I realise that if I said that you wouldn't take any notice!"

I nodded. We had not come all this way to stop in the snow on some God forsaken Scottish back lane. We had come for the record. We would take that record. We would take it on all fours if I had to. I would make it to John O'Groats. Nothing would stop me. The powers that be could throw anything at me but we would win through. And eventually, like the Gods on Olympus, they would look down and either relent or applaud the efforts of this poor ant-like creature crawling its way through the snow to the end of Britain.

"You can also try and walk on the right hand camber wherever possible" James added.

"I have my orthotic inserts I can put in my right shoe," I remembered. "They are for anti-pronation when the foot is in danger of turning inwards at the ankle. Putting that insert in would help tilt the foot and hence the leg to the right."

"Fine. Anything that will help shift the balance and try and get the patella back must be of help. Meanwhile let's do the standard ICE treatment - a cold icepack on the knee, massaging away some of the fluid before I bind it tightly, and let's keep it elevated while you eat."

"Yes, great." I tried to keep back the flood gates of emotional tears that threatened to overwhelm me. "We'll get there," I blurted as much to myself as to the others. They knew we all had to pull ourselves out of our crisis in the snow.

This was the real testing point, the valley of death into which Christian and Hopeful found themselves in Bunyan's Pilgrims Progress.

"A great darkness and horror fell upon Christian, so that he

could not see before him. Also here he in a great measure lost his senses so that he could neither remember nor orderly talk of any of those sweet refreshments that he had met with in the way of his pilgrimage. "

I looked out of the window at the covering of snow that lay all around. From a heatwave in the south of England where we were covering ourselves with ice cold water from a sponge to try and keep cool and couldn't get enough liquid inside of us, to a blizzard in the mountains and dinner in the snow! "I know records never come easily, but this is ridiculous!" I thought. "But we will make it. The record is ours for the taking. We shall be even prouder of our achievement. Nothing can stop us. "

I tried to control my emotions, fearful that my voice would shake with the pent up tensions. Doug's crew all clustered round looking at me, looking for a signal, looking for a lead. I put it quite simply:

"I'm afraid I can't run anymore. My right knee is just too painful and it will give way. I'm sorry. But we know what the problem is. We're going to have to rethink our approach. Let's have a look at the map. "

Ian gave me some marvellous pasta concoction and a hot drink. I asked James to do what he could with my feet. He carefully took off my shoes and socks and started to cut off the wrecked bandages. Doug sat down next to me. I sensed his calm, comforting strength. We looked at the map together.

"I think we're all a bit tired and emotional!" he said. "Now, let's have a look and decide what we've got to do. "

We had to dig ourselves positively out of the hole we were in. And dig we would, as a team. Together.

I reckoned we had between 120 and 130 miles to go. Although the worst of the hills were behind us, we still had quite a few left. If I couldn't run, then we had better play safe and assume a speed of no more than 4 mph. We had in fact done slightly more than that into the blizzard from Aviemore, but the last few miles had shown I could not necessarily keep that up.

I calculated we could still beat the record but we would have to cut down the overnight stops to play safe. I would also need even closer support with one of the vans hardly ever out of sight. It would require an even greater team effort. I explained my thoughts and asked them whether they were prepared to make that even greater effort. Of course I knew the answer. But the strength of their response and their commitment gave me a tremendous feeling that despite the trough we were in at the moment, there was no doubt about the end result. It would just take time.

It would also require great effort on my part. I would have to keep my concentration and my determination going. I would have very few breaks and must keep as steady a pace as possible. I must protect my right knee and my damaged left foot and just hope that things did not deteriorate too badly.

With largely new dressings, dry socks and shoes and some warm food and drink inside, I was lowered down onto the road and, oh so slowly and ever so painfully, put one foot in front of the other. It seemed to take me an age to move a hundred yards and my arms seemed to be moving more than my feet, as I kept pumping them to try and drive myself along.

Alone in the snow and perhaps slightly irreverently, the thought of Captain Oates on Scott's Antarctic expedition flashed into my mind. *"I'm going for a walk. I may be gone some time."* I smiled. Funny thing the mind to play a bit of a joke on you at a time like this. Perhaps it thinks it's all a bit of a game. Maybe it is. "Now, let's just do it."

Slowly I forced my body to raise its pace. *"When the going gets tough, the tough get going." "Let's see what you're made of."* I looked up into the whiteness of the softly falling snow in the midst of that quiet you get when you are alone in a snow covered landscape.

"God of Life,
Eternity cannot hold you,
nor can our little words catch the magnificence
of your kindness.
Yet in the space of our small hearts
And in silence, you can come and repair us."

I walked on the right hand side of the road. My knee held me. Thank God. It would be all right. It had to be.

When we rejoined the main road and looked down the slope ahead to Inverness, I knew however that I would not make it without some support. I remembered that first time I did a hundred miles in a running event at Chorley and could only complete with an upturned broom handle as a crutch. I now used Cyril's shoulder as that crutch and together we limped down the hill. I focused my whole body and mind on the bridge beyond Inverness which twinkled with lights out of the gloom. "We will make it. There's no need to fight. We're beyond that."

"The winds of grace blow all the time.
All we need to do is set our sails." (Ramakrishna)

The final vision is merely hypothetical if you cannot manage the intermediate steps and reach it.

While you may have a master plan, it must be capable of adaptation and of responding flexibly to changing circumstances.

The future is determined by the nature and quality of our thinking which must be clear and considered even under pressure.

"Our mind is the key to achievement." (David Hemery) But so are the hearts and minds of the team.

When the going gets tough, not only do the tough get going, but also the true quality and commitment of the team are tested to the ultimate. A crisis for a committed team will only enhance their cohesion and determination; everyone will appreciate their own particular contribution and the interdependency of the team.

Some managements try to manage by crisis and tension to maximise commitment. But there is a world of difference between managing by fear and managing via a positive partnership.

The role of a leader increasingly is to provide the environment where the skills and strength of the team can be freed and deployed to achieve the vision that all have agreed. Sometimes leaders have to let go and even lead from behind.

14

The Mind Takes Over

As you cross the suspension bridge onto the Black Isle north of Inverness, you see a name on the roadside sign that brings a spring to even the tiredest step: "John O'Groats."

A groat was an old coin and was evidently the cost of a ferry crossing from the mainland to the Orkney Islands that lie just off the northern coast of Scotland. John or Jan was the oarsman who would row you across. Jan de Grot was thought to have crossed from the Netherlands to Caithness in the latter part of the 15th Century. In fact, his own name and the place name probably derived from the currency he used. In Canisbay Church there is a sandstone slab commemorating various members of the de Grot family. Jan of the Groat was now on the map and each step brought him closer.

Amos had been stopped for a third time by the police. This time it was for waiting just before a turning on the main Inverness road to check we were ok. He had now gone ahead to get some rest and we agreed to phone him at midnight and tell him where we had got to for our intended short rest stop. But as I started the decent of the far side of the Black Isle towards the Cromarty Firth, I made the decision that was to ensure we broke the record and by a substantial margin.

I would not stop at midnight after all. I would instead walk right through the night and go for as long as possible the next day before collapsing for a half hour rest. I would then get up and go again until I could walk no further. We would eat on the move without lunch or dinner stops. Sleep deprivation would determine when I had to take a break and then it must be for no more than 30 minutes. I would stop where I collapsed and not before.

I told Doug of my decision and he and the crew agreed that they would of course support whatever I wanted. It would mean they would have to change the pattern of their own shift system and get less sleep themselves but they would manage.

I asked Doug to drive the van just a few yards behind me with its headlights on and to direct some suitably rousing music at me through the forward facing loud speaker, as we had done back in Devon on that first night. With James by my side, we picked up pace and walked under a starlight sky with the moon just rising down towards the dark expanse of the Cromarty Firth.

The Causeway below us was just a few feet above the water and does not give the appearance of a bridge at all. With virtually no lights on it, it looks as though you are just heading straight for the water with the intention somehow of floating over to the other side. The occasional light coming in our direction could have been a fishing boat rather than the headlights of a car crossing the causeway.

After we had finished the symphonies of Boyce on the CD player, we turned it off and just listened to the silence and felt the depth of the hills reflected in the wide expanse of water as it beckoned us towards the sea and on northwards.

Twenty-five miles north of Inverness, Don Thompson put on his rucksack, wished me all the best and disappeared back the way we had come. He had to catch the coach from Inverness back south. As a gardener, he had promised a client that he would only miss one Tuesday session. So now before dawn on Sunday, he was going for the coach that would ensure he returned eventually to Deal in Kent on Monday in good time to recover and prepare himself for his gardening appointment. Rather than hang around Inverness, he had decided to keep helping us for as long as possible and then get in a good training spin by walking back 25 miles in the night. I would miss his cheery smile and tremendous, if sometimes rather tiring, enthusiasm. Amos would no doubt miss having someone to organise!

Because we had known earlier that the second van would be reduced to just Amos and Derek once Don departed, Doug had asked Cyril to move across. It was as he joined me that I learned of his adventure with the new thermal vest.

Evidently as we moved north of Perth, everyone had started to feel the cold. Cyril had therefore invested in a new thermal top, which had kept him warm as we marched up and over Drumochter

Pass. During his rest stop around Aviemore, he had decided to wash it along with other kit and had loaded the lot into a local launderette. Too late, he remembered the advice of the sales lady: "Do not wash it or dry it on too hot a temperature. Otherwise...." The washing cycle had finished, but as the drying cycle began there was a faint smell of burning. This increased as the cycle progressed and Cyril could only watch as though on a TV screen as his new thermal top visibly shrank as it steamed gently behind the glass. When he could finally rescue it, the extra large vest suitable for a 44" chest, might just have fitted my nine year old daughter - or perhaps one of her larger teddies. So poor Cyril had had to battle into the blizzard and walk through the snow without the benefit of his expensive thermal top which was now paraded as a reminder to all of us of a need to follow the washing and drying instructions.

We were soon to witness another lesson, this time on van management. To make extra room in the van so I could crash out whenever necessary, Doug decided that all the bags should be stowed in the toilet/shower compartment. His van moved ahead of me and parked in a layby and Doug and James stowed the bags away as planned. As I approached, James switched on the water pump so I could have a refreshing sponge and clean my teeth as I passed by. However, shortly afterwards, water started pouring from the bottom of the van. As with other experiences, I just walked on and hoped all would be well. Doug and James dashed into the van to find out what had happened. The answer was quite simple. The toilet had flooded because the bags were standing on the flush pedal!

We were now in good walking country with the sea shining to the right of us, the mountains to the left and bright gorse and spring flowers all around. A few clouds threatened the occasional flurry of sleet, but generally the weather was set fair with the mountains largely sheltering us from the cold north westerly wind. The terrain was also fairly flat and the map suggested this would remain the case until we hit the ominously threatening hairpin bends around Helmsdale.

The early morning sun was shining on the sands around Dorloch Firth and the bridge which had been built since my last trip in 1988, saved us a few miles. My spirits rose. Each step now drew us nearer our destination and every sighting for the Guinness Book of Records by my crews, whether in car parks or small villages, produced enthusiastic claps of support. Everyone knew we were on record pace and enthusiastically spurred us on.

Some holidaymakers took a photograph of the banner on the back of one of the vans and cheered as I strode past. No doubt they would recount how they had seen and been part of our record-breaking adventure. I even found the energy to wave back and felt my smile spreading and relaxing my tired limbs.

By the time we reached Golspie some four hours later, I was however slowly sinking into sleep. I had gone from Drumochter Pass right through Saturday and Saturday night and now to Sunday lunchtime without any sleep and only two food stops (near Aviemore and in the snow near Moy, south of Inverness). I was feeling a bit like one of my ultra-distance running colleagues who, on a 48 hour run round a track, could not stop dreaming of the large double bed he passed each circuit and which looked so inviting. Eventually, he had to collapse onto it and its soft yellow eiderdown. He was immediately rescued by a couple of colleagues from the sandpit at the end of the long jump!

The van therefore pulled into a side turning just as we reached Golspie and I crashed out as soon as my head hit the pillow.

Exactly 30 minutes later, Doug gently told me it was time to get going and so off I went like some creature on auto-pilot, who did not have the capability to make decisions for himself.

Getting started was terrible. The pain underneath my left foot was almost unbearable and I could only inch myself along in a painful shuffle. I kept my eyes fixed firmly ahead trying to hold back tears of emotion and pain, fight tiredness and focus on the bend in the road at the end of the village. I had to blot out the signals coming from my feet.

At least my right knee was surviving pretty well. The relative flatness, my walking by and large on the right hand side of the road with the right hand camber, my orthotic device in my right shoe further shifting my stance and James's tight bindings keeping everything in place, seemed to be working. That was also a great mental release. It was now just a question of focusing on the road ahead and thinking of that sign "The Last House" at John O'Groats.

Slowly I began to swing my arms and force my legs to follow.

My mind somehow numbed the pain in my feet and I could again start to take in some of the scenery.

We passed the occasional "broch" (an old circular stone settlement) perched on the cliffs looking out to sea. We were also walking parallel to a railway line, although no trains passed us.

As we approached Helmsdale I walked more and more within myself, conserving my mental effort for what I knew would be both a painful descent and tiring climb along those hairpins.

I was not to be disappointed! The roadside warning said the descent was 13%. No doubt the climb on the other side was similar. With James's strong arm, I hobbled down the hill trying not to stride too much and hence put undue pressure on my knee. The village looked an ideal scenic rest stop if you were on a leisurely holiday. The cottages were brightly painted and looked friendly in the sunlight with a green valley to our left down which flowed the Helmsdale River into a harbour past a towered church. A few yards up the hill, we saw a cluster of bikes outside the youth hostel. As we approached, a welcoming party greeted us. We recognised the faces of some cyclists we had seen some miles back.

Earlier in the afternoon a couple of cyclists had stopped and walked with me. They were amazed that we would be doing the end-to-end in just over 10 days; that was the time they were targeting on their bikes! Their support vehicle had gone ahead with their gear and the two men in their mid-thirties were enjoying the last couple of days of their event. A third colleague was a few miles behind and slightly less athletic looking.

Their company for a mile or so was a refreshing break. They were so interested in our exploits and so full of praise and encouragement that they provided a spur to the afternoon's efforts. Relaying what we had done and how we had gone about our adventure reminded me that we were indeed engaged on a world-beating effort and should be proud of what we were achieving. I also reminded myself how fortunate we were to be walking along in the sunshine in good spirits and in reasonable physical condition after having done so many hundreds of miles. My support crew also enjoyed nattering to them. When they kindly put some money in one of our SPARKS buckets and cycled off waving, they said they would see us outside the Helmsdale Youth Hostel and hopefully the next morning at John O'Groats ..... if we were not

166

too fast!

So here they were, with others who were staying at the hostel, cheering and clapping as we started the assault of the long, and hopefully, last major climb.

I was surprised I did not remember any of this section from my 1988 event. Maybe I was then too tired and just looking at the road ahead to take in any of the scenery. In any case, it was perhaps just as well that I did not remember the seemingly unending climb. When you have been giving everything you have for so long and have lost a lot of muscle power, it seems cruel to have to face such a challenge so near the end.

I would have been encouraged had I heard the great shout that evidently went up from the other van crew, as they saw me attempting my assault on the hill. They knew the state of my knee and I suspect guessed the state of the rest of me! When they saw that I had made it down the 13% slope and was now giving it everything I had up the other side, they evidently burst into a spontaneous united shout and clapped with exhilaration. Their hearts and souls were so with me that as they passed with great waving and encouragement, I felt a new burst of determination.

But then near the top of the steep section, though with a more gentle slope to come, my right toe exploded. It was already just a large blister with the toenail floating on the top. Now the effort of the hill had resulted in the nail digging in and bursting the blister and pressing on into the raw flesh. I gave out a yelp and ground to a halt. I was stuck on the road unable to move forward or to stagger to one side to sit down.

The same thing had happened a couple of years earlier on the Paris-Colmar race. I was just five miles from the Epinal check-point with its one hour compulsory rest stop, had just passed one of the female French walkers and had told my medical crew to go on and meet us at the check-point, when my little toe went. The French female promptly overtook me and I lost over an hour crawling painfully those last five miles. Interestingly, Amos had also been in the accompanying van on that occasion.

He and James now came running down the hill with James's medical bag. They lifted me to the side of the road and sat me on a large stone slab. I kept saying "Oh no," and kept thinking "Not now. We're so near. Just hold it all together for a bit longer...

please."

We had just over 50 miles to go. For a moment those 50 miles seemed an impossibly long way. For some reason I said to Amos "I don't know if we'll make it." Amos glared back and gave me the answer I expected: "Rubbish. We haven't come all this way to stop within sight of the finish. Just tell yourself that."

Of course he was right. Deep down I believed what he had said. Maybe I only made the statement to hear his answer. I would have been worried if he had not responded vigorously. I felt ashamed I had even uttered a doubt and hoped Amos would not tell anyone. Somehow I sensed he knew exactly how I felt, knew why I had said what I had said and would not let on. Such was the closeness we had all achieved. We just "knew" without speaking all that mattered, how we felt and how we would together make it.

As I sat staring out to sea as James got to work, I felt as though I had been stripped mentally bare down to the raw essence of self. There was nothing to hide behind. No artificial pleasantries or polite screen of conversation protected me. I was laid bare and couldn't make the effort to hide anything. I said and showed what I thought, how I was. I felt frail and exposed collapsed there by the roadside. I was down to 10½ stone (145 pounds) despite eating and drinking regularly. The wind now made me shiver as I felt the loss of body weight.

But I had to haul myself over 50 more miles. I thought of what we had achieved so far; of the 780 miles we had already done. Just 50 to go; just one more night; just over this last hill and then you've cracked it; just one final great effort. I had to do it. There was no other way.

James had put some antiseptic ointment on the stump of my toe and bound it so it would not rub against the next toe. We cut the right shoe open even more so it could let the toe hang out. Both shoes were now cut in various places but had enough material left to hold themselves together. I asked James and Amos to lift me onto the road. I sensed them only half look at me once both feet were planted. They knew I did not want them watching me in my embarrassed state of naked pain. I tested my poor feet yet again on the hill.

Slowly I picked up speed and Amos went up the hill ahead of me. As I passed him alone at the back of his van, he smiled and gave a clenched fist sign of determination and encouragement. We didn't need to say a word. He knew I was repeating what he had said to me earlier. Both of us knew that the mind was intact and that the body would do what it was told. Inwardly I thanked Amos and half smiled back. A tear of released emotion trickled down my cheek and I brushed it away and focused on the emerging crest of the road ahead.

A few miles on and a lorry driver coming towards us pulled over into the side of the road. He waved and shouted encouragement and asked how many days we had been going. My crew went over to natter to him and found out that he had passed us two or three times on his journey from Perth to Wick delivering animal feed stuff. He also volunteered a couple of quid for our SPARKS bucket and with a sneezing of airbrakes and a loud toot he drove away. I realised that we would be in John O'Groats before he was back in Perth.

It was dark as we approached the radio masts on the hill above Wick. The lights on them never seemed to get any nearer. It was like looking at Blackpool Tower on the Manchester to Blackpool race walk. Fatal. The tower never gets any nearer.

Earlier, I had asked Doug to drive just behind me with the music blaring to help keep me awake. But after a few miles at under five miles per hour, the van had given up the ghost and the electrics had gone again. With no lights, Doug pulled into the side of the road and phoned Amos to find out his position and ask him to take over. As Doug's back was turned, Amos pulled up behind him into the same layby and took great pleasure in informing Doug of his position over the phone!

Amos's stint with the music did not last much longer than Doug's. Despite the increasingly cold north westerly wind, his van boiled over after a couple of hours at such a slow pace. So we reverted to Amos leap-frogging along the road and Derek and Cyril walking with me.

Without the music and with the lights of the Wick aerials still getting no closer, it was increasingly difficult for me to force myself to keep moving at a decent pace. We were also now exposed on a ridge and the north westerly wind was bitingly cold. Amos heated drinks as best he could and kept darting across the road to give them to me. But as I slowed with the wind and through tiredness, I just got colder and colder. I put on someone's quilted jacket and thermal mittens. Cyril and Derek walked either side to stop me falling over in my tiredness, as I began to stagger on the road.

Eventually, we drew parallel with the radio aerials and could see some lights ahead which suggested Wick was not too far. I had promised myself a sit down when we could see Wick. But I was by now only just capable of staggering to the back of the van and being pushed up and into its warm embrace. I was so cold and my hands in particular were freezing. I knew my feet must also be frozen, especially as the shoes had been cut away in so many places so the toes could poke through. They were now exposed to the elements and the renewed sleet which was hitting us. At least in their cold state my feet were anaesthetized.

I asked what we had to warm my hands and Cyril gave me the kettle. I collapsed on the seat with my hands around the kettle and my head in a cardboard box of music tapes. Cyril and Amos promptly threw two sleeping bags over me.

After half an hour, they woke me, gave me some warm rice pudding and lowered me down out of the van. It was my second half hour sleep in 46 hours. We had under 20 miles to go and just 17 miles once we reached the centre of Wick. I inched off in the direction of the lights with dawn just breaking.

From Wick the road to John O'Groats is tediously flat across treeless, windswept moorland. There is one village and a Victorian French chateau-style castle, but otherwise there is little to relieve the monotony. However, with both vans together, our little procession slowly made its way towards our long dreamed of goal. Chewing Power Bars all the way to keep up my energy, I warmed as the early sun broke intermittently through the clouds.

We crested the last little hill and there before us lay the cluster of buildings by the edge of a calm blue sea dotted with islands. The Orkneys shimmered in the sun-splashed sea. What a marvellous sight. My whole body and soul sighed. I shook Doug's hands, as we let the vans charge ahead like animals released from their leads. On they sped, down the hill to the hotel and the shop with that sign we all longed to see "John O'Groats. The Last House."

The crews parked the vans and got a tourist to sign the last sighting we would need for the Guinness Book of Records.

At 8.25 am and 35 seconds I touched the magic sign and a great cheer went up. From somewhere a bottle of champagne was produced and thrust into my hand. I felt as though I should have shaken it and sprayed myself, the crews and everyone else in sight. We had done it. We had together come 830 miles all the way from Lands End in 10 days 2 hours and 25 minutes. I had taken over 15 hours off my previous time in 1988 and over 13 hours off Don Ritchie's record. 13 hours was a respectable amount!

I shook hands and hugged every member of my world-beating crew and thanked them again and again.

We would celebrate that evening in a nearby restaurant and relive the stories that would be engrained in our minds and emotions for ever. Every yard of the road from Lands End now had a special significance. Every scene, every village, every town would never be the same again. Neither would we. A special bond had been forged between all of us.

"By your deeds shall ye be known," it says somewhere in the Bible. What deeds we had together accomplished and shaped. We had pushed out the boundaries of what can be achieved. We had tested ourselves near to the limit and proved to ourselves what we were capable of doing. We all stood that bit prouder as a result.

There is a Himalayan saying: *"It is better to have lived one day as a tiger than a thousand years as a sheep."*

We had chosen to live for 10 days as tigers.

Three days later Sandra touched the same post beneath that magical announcement:

"John O'Groats   The Last House."

Only two from her original crew had been able to stay to the finish. I had met Sandra at almost the same spot where we had had our crisis in the snow and had taken back 2 of her crew and left Derek and Cyril with her. They were to prove just as committed to help Sandra achieve her objective as they had been helping me.

It had been a calm reunion between us as I headed back South and Sandra continued on her painful way North. We both knew there was no point or time for great emotion. She still had a job to do.

She ate her meal in the van and I sat next to her. She repeated to me the phrases she must have said over and over to herself and her crew. "I'm going to get there." "The time doesn't matter, I'm just going to get there." I gave her a big hug and felt some of the emotion shaking her. She wiped her eyes, put on her sandals (her feet were too bad to take any shoes) and said with the determination which signified she meant business:

"Right!"

She lowered herself onto the slush covered road, put on her gloves and said, "Who's coming with me?" Boyd, as always, answered the call and we stood watching the pair set off down the road towards Inverness.

On reflection, it was rather a bizarre sight. Boyd is about the same height and build as Sandra but has his hair cut almost skin-head short. He was still in shorts even in the slush and, looked like a well trained chimpanzee. He led off with a water bottle in his hand. Sandra fell in behind dressed in woolly hat, long anorak, and long trackster trousers but yet wore sandals on her feet.

After a few minutes, her one van set off to track this odd looking couple and see her safely to her long awaited and so richly deserved goal. The group of us left on the roadside waved goodbye and then got back into our own van and with my other van, like the inseparable twins they had been for 10 days, we headed off south.

In between drifting off to sleep and looking at the views, some of which we had seen as we made our rather slower progress up the country, I thought of what we had done.

My mind went back to that apparently casual question to Doug as to whether he might be our team manager. His positive response had given life to the vision Sandra and I had set but could not realise. It was as though the road to a vision on the hill had a six foot wide trench dug across it right in front of us. It is no good having the vision if you have no way of taking the first step.

I remembered how we had crafted the objectives and thought of the stakeholders that needed to be satisfied and what their interests would be. How our management structure had deliberately left the charity to organise their own fundraising, with support from us, but not in a way which distracted us from our single-minded focus to

172

set new records. The clear leadership role assigned to Doug and the van leaders under him and then to every member of the team - including financial controller back at base - had been important in establishing responsibilities and involvement from everyone and a feeling that each member of the team was important. Delegation did indeed free individuals to give of their best.

The milestones set had been valuable guides along the implementation path. It is no good having great aspirations without not only the commitment of the team but also a practical plan with quantifiable points which you know have to be reached before you can take the next step. Getting the various skills together to make a cohesive team was perhaps the most important and most difficult task. Having to accept compromises and to be flexible on the details was also a lesson well learnt. The perfect enduring organisational structure does not exist. It needs constantly to be adapted to meet changing demands.

As the adventure unfolded so having an established routine and pattern where everyone knew what was expected had proved vital. Even so the maintenance of team motivation and enthusiasm relied a great deal not only on team chemistry built on confidence and belief in what they were doing, but also feedback from myself and communication between the teams.

When the crisis came, it was our ability to respond flexibly with utter determination and commitment which saw us reach our goal. The management lesson that the pursuit of excellence requires innovation and the capability to respond flexibly was so simply demonstrated.

There are lessons there for every organisation and every individual. Most of them are simple and obvious. That does not mean to say they are followed even by those that consider themselves amongst the best.

At about 5.00 pm on 18th May the phone rang in our London flat. Sandra had made it at one minute past four that afternoon. She had taken nearly 8 hours off the ladies record. Her time was 13 days 10 hours 1 minute. She had walked all the way after the first day with appalling feet, stomach problems, a fever in Scotland

and many other untold problems. It was a supreme example of mind over matter. An awesome display of mental focus and determination.

The Guardian newspaper well summarised the adventure:

"Richard Brown is not the craziest runner in the world, although he did take 13 hours off the Land's End to John O'Groats record this week. That title surely belongs to his wife, Sandra, who completed the 830 mile course yesterday to break the women's record by nearly 8 hours."

Crazy, or just committed, or both?

15

Who is the Winner

Winning experiences are seldom about world records and Olympic medals. Those are in any case only the outward signs and outward recognition of performances that are intensely personal. It is the personal sense of achievement that provides the lasting satisfaction, the real winning experience.

A record can be broken the following week. A medal is only as meaningful as the quality of the competition on the day.

The Americans boycotted the Moscow Olympics and others boycotted the Los Angeles Games. In so doing, they debased the value of the medals won. They also devalued the Olympic spirit itself. They could not however devalue the sense of personal achievement which individuals felt as they judged themselves against their own potential and their own aspirations.

Any individual of whatever age knows when he or she has performed well. The resulting satisfaction may come from a performance on the athletics track or on the stage. It may come from a written report at work or from helping old people one evening a week at a nursing home. Whatever the external object or source of our satisfaction, it is the internal feeling which gives us the inner glow.

External recognition is of course nice. Few of us would shun or reject it. It helps our self confidence to know that others also recognise a job well done and it can help encourage us not to give up when others are looking on. But we know the real worth of our achievement. We know how much we have put in, what difficulties or obstacles we have overcome, and how the result compares against our expectations and the standards we set.

We can almost ignore the views of others insofar as they are immaterial to our own views of ourselves and our achievements. Only we know how well we have performed against the objectives and standards we have set.

Even in an athletics event, the objective may not be an athletics output. I remember how one of our friends, James Zarei, stopped to help a colleague on the Spartathlon race from Athens to Sparta. He could have improved his own time and position in the race. But he chose, perhaps in the true spirit which originally fired the Greek Olympic Games, to support his struggling friend. They crossed the line together with a camaraderie that spoke wonders for the spirit behind the race and behind so much of human endeavour. James also, I know, got greater satisfaction from that race than from many others. Being competitive and succeeding in the outer world and in the eyes of others is not of itself sufficient.

"A great champion is he who does not care for the result of the race - whether he is first or last or in between. He races just to get joy and give joy to the observers. " (Sri Chinmoy)

Sandra has some of this quality beneath her undoubted competitive drive. She is one of the great ambassadors for British sport because she goes out of her way to smile and acknowledge the enthusiasm and support of those around her. People often want to associate with those undertaking an adventure, but sometimes find the competitor too competitive, too focused, not at all responsive to those wishing him or her well and offering encouragement on the way.

On the Paris-Colmar walk Sandra has deliberately kept up her good humour. Partly no doubt this is self reinforcing and encourages her belief that all is going well, but also it motivates her team and gives pleasure to the many onlookers. When through tiredness her hands could not wave, she made certain one of her crew responded to the well wishers while she continued to smile through adversity. Is it any wonder that she makes such friends wherever she goes and that people remember with pleasure her exploits?

The same approach was apparent on the Forrest Gump Run. Not complaining, despite her difficulties, she tried to maintain her cheerfulness. Whenever I let my mind relax and stop fighting against the weather, my tiredness or my inner self, then I experienced a similar tranquillity. To take delight in everything around you is to gain inspiration and to undertake a pilgrimage where the journey is more important than the final arrival.

176

The winner is also someone who has not only come to terms with the result, whatever that might be, but has also set out from the start with that objective. In a marathon or shorter run, more often than not these are the people in the second half of the race, they are the people who are not fighting for places and positions but rather who are enjoying the experience of being on the road with others, taking delight in what is around them and being only too pleased to make it to the finish. You see it in their smiles, as they encourage each other (winners are seldom loners). The large ladies, the family out together, the person in the wheelchair or dressed as a Donald Duck collecting money for a charity in a large, yellow bucket. These are the winners; these are the people with whom onlookers relate. They give joy and receive joy. They have competed in the spirit of friendship and have maintained it right through to the finish. Their sense of self fulfilment will probably be greater than many who have finished numerically "ahead" in the race.

When I am out training, I am not so much impressed by the sleek athlete bounding along, especially if that person is in fancy posing athletics gear, as by the overweight or the elderly. I wonder if I would have the guts to turn out and plod round if I were overweight, my flesh bouncing up and down no doubt to the occasional caustic remarks or thoughts of onlookers. I wonder if I will still be motivated enough to keep going when I am in my seventies. These people are winners because they have had to overcome physical and metal obstacles to achieve their objective. They have a deeper sense of wanting to achieve than the sleek 20 year old for whom a jog in the park is no great sweat.

Every winner converts the difficult to the feasible. As they grow in confidence and resolve they convert the seemingly impossible to the possible. They go through the valley of death and come out the other side to achieve the self imposed challenge which they themselves have set. They stretch themselves to their limits and in so doing stretch our achievements as a species that bit further.

If we ever stop pushing out our limits, whether as individuals or as a species, then we will cease to have a purpose. We will begin that long slow death in which our abilities and potential waste away through non-use. *"If you don't use it you lose it."*

As we push out our frontiers, so we also delve deeper into ourselves. As we run the outer race, so we also proceed in the inner race. Each individual is running towards a destination which is unique. The vision may be far away on the distant hill. But as we slowly approach, we have that strange sense that the vision is not only getting nearer but is actually itself coming to meet us. Soon we have embraced our vision in our mind and it appears right in front of us. We are almost there mentally, it is just our body that has to catch up.

Sri Chinmoy has the lovely description of Gawinda/God/the Great I Am running with us just a couple of feet in front. We are encouraged to keep going because he is just there, encouraged to go that bit further and even reach out and touch him. He will not let us down or let us fall.

Sometimes in life as in a race we can forget this and strive too much. The Chandogya Upanishad has one of the most poignant images to convey the sense of profound peace which can be achieved:

"As a tethered bird grows tired of flying
About in vain to find a place of rest
And settles down at last on its own perch,
So the mind, tired of wandering about
Hither and thither, settles down at last
In the Self, to which it is bound.
All creatures have their source in him.
He is their home; he is their strength."

As we get closer to our objective, we get closer to ourselves. We move into a higher state of being. We feel that the goal is within us. Finally, we realise that not only is the goal within us, but that we are the goal itself. *"Your own higher self is the goal that your lower self has been searching for."*

It is this higher purpose this sense of oneness which I have tried to allude to many times in this book. Some writers imagine that "success" is all about making money in the material world. Their motives are narrow, even selfish.

Let the dogs fight over the bones and spoils. We have the potential for better, higher, more worthy objectives.

The pursuit of excellence should be the pursuit of the wholly satisfying. The holistic excellence may mean an apparent

178

compromise of the athletic excellence because other things are seen as important in achieving a balance. More likely however, recognition and development of these other attributes enhances and enriches the achievement of excellence. *"The mind and body become one"* (David Hemery); *"Suddenly it was as though I woke up and noticed that I had somehow been on a different level of consciousness."* (Ayrton Senna)

Winning a race, achieving market leadership, doubling recruitment at a club become not ends in themselves but part of a greater, more satisfying and longer lasting objective. Our potential is seldom so focused that it can be realised in one area of life. We may start with that focus, but we will soon realise our potential is much greater and that even to achieve lasting satisfaction in that one area requires us to develop our other attributes. It is like the athlete who realises that he cannot just develop one set of muscles. He must develop the balancing set at the same time.

As we progress, so we have the opportunity and the enjoyment of discovering new possibilities, new opportunities, new challenges. We must take time to stand back and assess that potential. There is a great danger that all of us are too busy coping with what is urgent to think about what is important.

We can so easily proceed along the well trodden path, like Moses tending the sheep in Gideon until he is faced with the burning bush. Our inner fire which burns away our old assumptions and fears must constantly be re-stoked. We must continually recharge ourselves with renewed enthusiasm, zeal and a mission in life.

As we run the outer and inner race, *"Try to be a true athlete and try all the time to surpass and go beyond all that is bothering you and standing in your way. Be a real winner so that ignorance, limitation and imperfection will all drop far behind you in the race."* (Sri Chinmoy)

Our race will never be won. But along the way we can enjoy and share so many winning experiences. The opportunities are there for us to seize. It is for us to decide how much of our potential we want to realise. In that sense, "The only limitations are mental."

"Life and sports cannot be separated; they are one. We are running in the outer world and the inner self."

On the Forrest Gump Run, I believe every member of the team experienced "A uniquely satisfying adventure" - the objective we had set. The records Sandra and I achieved were also their records. Everyone contributed in their own way to that team effort. Each one experienced something special on the long road as part of a closely knit team in cramped conditions. Each one knows what that was.

We all came to appreciate a little of the power and potential of the mind, of the body, of the whole self:

"Smaller than a grain of rice, smaller than a grain of barley, smaller than a mustard seed, smaller than a grain of millet, smaller even than the kernel of a grain of millet is the Self. This is the Self dwelling in my heart, greater than the earth, greater than the sky, greater than all the worlds." (Chandogya)

We shall tell our children and hopefully grandchildren about our great adventure. Every time we go through a village or town on the route, or even cross the road which we trod, the memories will return and the place will forever have a special significance.

"We shall not cease from exploration.
And the end of all our exploring
Will be to arrive where we started
And know the place for the first time." (T S Eliot)

We also know the intensely personal inner experience, the experience "too deep for tears." The intensity of a winning experience is related to the length and intensity of the afterglow.

We do not however intend to sit down in our armchairs and be warmed by this afterglow for the rest of our lives. There are other challenges and new adventures awaiting us. New visions are there on new hills in front of us. The excitement of life is never over. Sandra and I are now planning our next *"winning experience."*

Acknowledgements

My greatest thanks go to those to whom this book is dedicated. Without a team effort no individual success is achievable.

I would also like to thank Colin Turner whose best selling book *"Born to Succeed"* should be the inspiration to others it was to me. Our colleague, Ffyonna Cambell's compelling reads *"Feet of Clay"* and *"On Foot through Africa"* make our ordeals seem ordinary. Without the financial support from the "Forrest Gump" video distributors CIC and their MD, James Harding, the adventure would never have started. Countrywide Communications were the catalyst that brought us together, and I particulary applaud Claire Donnelly who then drove with us arranging media coverage in between finding her way on a pocket sized atlas. Hugh Peers and Angela Dudley at SPARKS (Sports Aiding Medical Research for Kids) looked after the fund raising and encouraged us, while Sally Gunnell and Steve Cram recorded messages of support for SPARKS. Numerous other individuals and organisations (eg: Westcountry Motorhomes and the Talbot Hotel, Leominster) gave support and I hope are fully acknowledged in the text.

This book would not have been written without the massive typing and retyping effort put in by Vivien Fowler at Sue Sheppard - The No 1 Staff Bureau in Bristol. Richard Ireland at Strange and Dawson Advertising, Bristol, designed the cover and laid out the photographs in his usual pleasant and professional manner. Keith Kirkland at Redwood Books (part of Bath Press) gave invaluable advice on the printing.

But I finish where I began with admiration for the commitment and enthusiasm of our support crews in a great team effort, and of course to the most committed partner one could ever imagine, my wife and many times record holder, Sandra.

Appendix 1 - The Route

MAIN RD NO	NAME ON SIGNPOST	DIVERSION	TOWN MAP
A30	Penzance	Thro Town Centre	Yes
A30	Redruth	Thro Hayle TC B3301 (ignore Portreath) continue to A30	No
A30	Redruth	TL Mt Pleasant Thro Bodmin TC rejoin A30	Yes
A30	Launceston	Ignore Polyphant route bypass Launceston	
A30	Okehampton	Bypass Okehampton at Stockley Hamlet TL for Belstone Corner. TR B3215 BR A3072 at Bow TR Coleford ST thro to A377 TR Crediton shortly after TL Pounds Hill Creedy Bridge TL A3072 Tiverton Bear East in Tiverton rejoin A373 at Cowleymoor	No
A373	Sampford Peverell	TL Uplowman Via Pitt st on to A300	
A38	Taunton	bypass Wellington thro Taunton rejoin A38	Yes
A38	Bridgwater	A38 thro Bridgwater	No
A38	Bristol	In Bristol TL Ashton Gate over River Avon	

A4	Avonmouth (M5)	TR Valley Rd take Clifton Down Rd follow A4018 Via Westbury on Trym under M5 take B4055 TR A403 to M4	Yes
	Toll Bridge	TL over Severn Bridge foot-bridge TR A466	
A466	Monmouth	TR Brockweir, take Offa's Dyke path (disused rly on o/s map) To Bigswear Br st over A466 take parallel road Rejoin A466 Redbrook	
A466	Hereford	TL A49 small detour L to Callow	
A49	Hereford	thro Hereford	Yes
A49	Leominster	TL B4361 Leominster Thro Leominster Thro Ludlow rejoin A49	
A49	Shrewsbury	bypass Church Stretton thro Shrewsbury Take A528 in TC At Harmer Hill Tr B5476 Thro Wem Thro Whitchurch Join A49	Yes
A49	Warrington	after Tiverton, (junction with A51) st on B5152 via Eaton & Cotebrook TR A49	
A49	Warrington	over M56 thro Warrington	Yes
A49	Preston	At Winwick take A573 Thro Golborne Thro Ince in Makerfield	

		Rejoin A49 under M6 TL immediately. See Map A6 thro Preston	Yes
A6	Lancaster	TR B6430 Thro Garstang Rejoin A6 A6 thro Lancaster *Runners-via Parliam. St* *and Skerton Br* *Vans-via Greyhound Br* *and TR A589* Both rejoin A6	Yes
A6	Kendal	after Levens Hall at junc *Runners-st on* *Vans-TL then R* Both rejoin A6 Join A591	
A591	Kendal	rejoin A6 Thro Kendal	
A6	Penrith	thro Penrith *Care - Different routes* *for vans & runners*	Yes
A6	Carlisle	thro Carlisle *Care - Different routes* join A7	Yes
A7	Hawick	thro Langholme thro Hawick	No Yes

A7	Galashiels	thro Selkirk
		See map for detour
		OPTIONS
		1.Take dismantled rly
		2.Take A7 to Bowland TL
		  then R to Dryburn.
		  Follow to Heriot House.
		  BL to N Middleton
		  Rejoin A7
		3.Take A7
			Yes

A7	Edinburgh	TL B704 TL A768 First R Liberton	

A7	Edinburgh	over A720 TL B701 via Colinton in Sighthill TR then L - Still B701 TL A90	
A90	Forth Rd Br	Over bridge TL B981 N TL B917 at Cowdenend after Kelty st on to B996 TL B996 Thro Kinross on B996 at A91 junc at Milnathort TR (B996) BL B996 TL Netherton via Duncrievie to Glenfarg rejoin B996 TL Scarhill via Blairstruie via Newbiggin to Bridge of Earn TL B912 thro Perth take A9 TL B867 Bankfoot Take lane between B867 and A9 Rejoin A9	Yes Yes
A9	Newtonmore	Stay on A9 thro Pitlochry on A924 Rejoin A9 at Kingussie TR B9152 before Aviemore rejoin A9	Yes
A9	Inverness	A9 thro Inverness At Kildary TL Lamington To Tain Rejoin A9	Yes
A9	Wick	Bypass Tain thro Wick to John O'Groats	No Yes

Appendix 2 - The Cost

FINAL INCOME AND EXPENDITURE

INCOME	£	£
Richard Brown	3500.00	
Countrywide	5000.00	
Westcountry Motors	500.00	
		9000.00

EXPENDITURE

Motor Vans:		
Westcountry	1989.80	
Knightcott	2540.00	
Fuel:	1065.78	
Other Travel	477.95	
Subsistence	1431.23	
Accommodation	153.25	
Sundry (Stationery/'phone)	547.18	
Medical	493.40	
Exceptional Items	124.74	
Total Expenditure		8823.33
Funds due to R Brown		176.67

Appendix 3 - List of Food at Start

2 Pkts instant mash	1 Marmite	2 Tins veg Peas/Carrot
3 pkts soup-thick	1 Pkt Mars Bars	1 Coffee Mate
3 pkts soup-thin	1 Tinned Apricots	3 Wholemeal bread
2 Tins tuna	1 Dried Dates	1 White sliced bread
2 Tins sardines	1 Dried mixed fruit	2 Lettuce
2 tins salmon	1 Pkt pasta	12 Tomatoes
6 Tins baked beans	1 Pkt pasta stir fry	2 Malt loaf
1 Tin Oak ham	2 Tins stew	1 Pkt sticky buns
2 Rice pudding	4 Toilet rolls	1 Jamaica ginger cake
2 Custard	3 Kitchen rolls	24 Bananas
2 Semolina	1 Pkt bin liners	6 Oranges
Macaroni	2 Soaps	6 Apples
1 Weetabix/Bran	1 Washing up liquid	1 Cottage cheese
Flakes/Muesli	4 Fruit juices	1 Edam/1 Cheddar
1 Box Tea bags	2 Long life milk	2 Large Yoghurt
1 Instant Coffee	2 Tinned tomatoes	fruit & plain
2 White sugar	1 Cooking oil	2 Pkts bacon
2 Low fat drink Choc	1 Salt & pepper	1 Low fat marg
1 Honey/Strawberry	1 Digestive biscuits	18 eggs
Jam/Marmalade	1 Ready Brek	3 Pizza

Appendix 4 - Typical Sighting Form

THE GUMP RUN

Lands End to John O'Groats

record attempt by Richard Brown - May 1995

I confirm I have seen the person in the photograph trying to break this record and raise money for SPARKS (Sports Aiding Research for Kids).

Name [please print]	Address	Place Where Seen	Time & Date

Appendix 5 - SPARKS

Our chosen charity was SPARKS (Sports Aiding Medical Research for Kids). This national charity was founded by top sports personalities to help alleviate suffering in children. Funds are raised through a wide range of fun sporting events to finance medical research projects at hospitals and universities throughout Britain.

SPARKS aims to help children to be born healthy and stay healthy.

Since 1991, SPARKS has pledged over £2.5 million to medical research projects including research into premature births (at Bristol Royal Infirmary), bone disease, muscle paralysis and childhood infections.

Further information on events and how you can become involved is available from the SPARKS national HQ:

SPARKS, Francis House, Francis Street, London SW1P 1DE

Appendix 6 - The Institute of Human Development

The Institute of Human Development was founded by the best selling author, business mentor and conference speaker, Colin Turner. His books include *"Born to Succeed"* and *"The Eureka Principle."*

The Institute has developed programmes which can help release the potential and enhance the performance of organisations and teams. Businesses such as BT, Hewlett Packard and IBM, as well as smaller companies, have successfully used them.

Richard Brown makes multimedia presentations on "The Winning Experience" under the aegis of the Institute to organisations, and at reduced rates for charity fund-raising events.

For more information on the programmes and presentations available, contact Colin or Richard at:

Burnts House, Chelwood, BS18 4NL